GO ▶ *climb*

Nigel Shepherd

London, New York, Munich, Melbourne, Delhi

Project Editor **Richard Gilbert**
Project Art Editor **Mark Cavanagh**
DTP Designer **Vania Cunha**
Production Controller **Melanie Dowland**
Managing Editor **Stephanie Farrow**
Managing Art Editor **Lee Griffiths**

Produced for Dorling Kindersley by
KAB Design, London
Design **Beverley Speight, Nigel Wright**
Editorial **Liz Dean**
Photography **Gerard Brown**

DVD produced for Dorling Kindersley by
Chrome Productions www.chromeproductions.com
Director **Gez Medinger**
Camera **Neil Gordon**
Production Manager **Portia Mishcon**
Production Assistant **Andrew Needham**
Voiceover **Josh Connor**
Voiceover Recording **Mark Maclaine**
Music **Chad Hobson**

Please note: Both metric and imperial measurements are given throughout this book, except for ropes, which are measured in millimetres and metres everywhere in the world.

First published in Great Britain in 2006 by
Dorling Kindersley Limited
80 Strand
London WC2R 0RL

A Penguin Company

2 4 6 8 10 9 7 5 3 1

Copyright © 2006 Dorling Kindersley Limited

A CIP catalogue record for this book is available from the British Library.

ISBN-13: 978-1-40531-502-9
ISBN-10: 1-4053-1502-4

Colour reproduction by Icon Reproduction, UK
Printed and bound in China by Hung Hing

Discover more at

www.dk.com

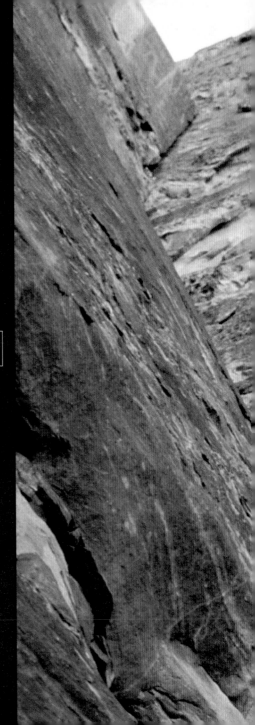

contents

how to use this book and DVD

This fully integrated book and accompanying DVD are designed to inspire you to get out onto the rock face. Watch all the essential techniques on the DVD in crystal-clear, real-time footage, with key elements broken down in state-of-the-art digital graphics, and then read all about them, and more, in the book.

Using the book

Venturing onto the rock for the first time can seem a daunting prospect, so this book explains everything you need to know to go climbing with safety and confidence. Cross-references to the DVD are included on pages that are backed up by footage.

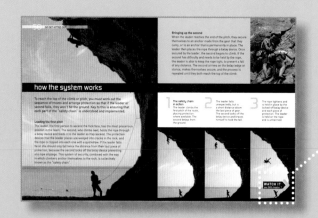

Switch on the DVD

When you see this logo in the book, check out the action in the relevant chapter of the DVD.

Using the DVD

Supporting the book with movie sequences and computer graphics, the DVD is the perfect way to see key techniques demonstrated in precise detail. Navigate to each subject using the main menu, and view sequences as often as you like to see how it's done!

Flick to the book

When you see this logo on the DVD, flick to the relevant page of the book to read all about it.

why climb?

In its simplest
form, rock climbing pits
the skills and strength of an
individual against a seemingly
vertical, slabby, or overhanging wall
of blank rock. Add to that a perceived,
and very occasionally real, element of
danger, and you have a unique combination
of elements that is testing both physically and
mentally. To be perched high on a rock face, with
fingers curled around a rough, positive handhold of rock,
and feet gripping onto toe-sized ledges, can be an exquisite
experience. Rope and protection equipment will keep you and
your partner safe, who shares every moment of the climb.

In this book, you will see how to take your first steps into this vertical
world. Learn how to tie the knots that link you to your rope, rock, and
partner, and find out how to move efficiently using all manner of hand
and footholds. We'll show you the equipment and clothing you'll need
to make it all happen in comfort. We'll explain all the essentials so
that you can go out there, have the satisfaction of discovering
more for yourself, and hopefully enjoy a long, rewarding
association with this unique sport.

Be safe. Have fun!

Nigel Shepherd

go for it

coming up...

Pleasures of movement: 18–21

In climbing, you'll enjoy the sensation of moving over rock and the physical challenge this presents – using the strength in feet, legs, hands, and arms to balance and move – along with the mental game of keeping calm in an unfamiliar and at times scary environment.

Climbing styles: 22–27

Rock climbing offers a range of climbing styles to suit your ability and aspirations. From "pure" trad climbing to sport climbing and bouldering, here is an overview of the unique techniques different climbing styles use.

Places to climb: 28–37

Climbing takes place in some of the most beautiful places on earth, but before you venture outdoors, indoor climbing centres provide safe learning zones for beginners. When you are ready, you can explore the world of climbing on every conceivable rock face, and learn the unique features and challenges that different rock types present – from sandstone and gritstone to rhyolite, limestone, and granite.

the rewards of climbing

Much of the satisfaction and reward of climbing lies in the pleasures of physical movement over rock. The variety of body positions, footholds, and handholds is infinite. You don't need to be a superhuman athlete to experience the joy of hanging on to a huge handhold or feeling rough rock beneath your feet.

On easy climbs handholds are generally plentiful, although it may not seem so at the time. The choice will depend largely on what holds you are strong enough to use in terms of gripping on and pulling yourself up. But climbing is not just about handholds. Your legs are stronger than your arms, so to climb more efficiently you should use your feet wisely. The lower the angle of the rock face, the easier it is to stand on your feet. Often there may appear to be very little to stand on, so you have to resort to smearing your feet over the rock surface (see page 70). Climbing shoes have sticky rubber soles, enabling you to grip well enough to bear weight on your feet on apparently very smooth rock.

Planning ahead

- Climbing can be like playing chess: you know what you want to do, but you need to re-evaluate your plan often, especially if your opponent (the rock face) surprises you. Never be afraid to back off slightly to take a second look at the problem.
- Breaking down a climb into manageable sections and resting between them lets you focus on the immediate problem rather than worrying about what lies ahead.
- Concentrate on taking the strain off your arms and resting them whenever you can. Lower-angle climbs offer more resting opportunities than steep routes.

pleasures of movement

developing your skills

At easier grades, climbing is a game in which you can concentrate fully on the moves in front of you. As you progress through the grades and become more proficient, other aspects require consideration. If you are the leader, factors such as arranging protection can prove frustrating, but they are an essential part of the whole experience.

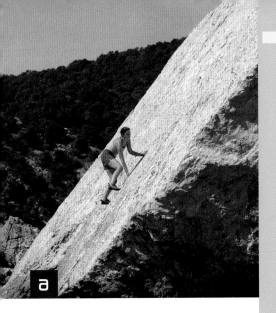

The challenges of tougher climbing

As you progress through the grades you may find yourself on a climb that is considerably steeper than you have previously attempted. You not only have to contend with the technical difficulty of working out the sequence of moves, but you will also need to gauge whether you have enough power in your legs, hands, fingers, and arms to sustain you through those moves. Without training the unique muscles you use in climbing, it is difficult to rely wholly on natural strength, and your knowledge of specific climbing techniques becomes important. You need to remember to build rest opportunities into your move sequences whenever possible, otherwise early forays on to steeper ground may leave you panting and puffing, wasting valuable energy that would be better expended on the moves required.

a Making progress
The satisfaction you gain from solving all elements of the puzzle is as rewarding mentally as the climb can be physically.

b Looking ahead
Take a good look at the route up the rock before you set off, noting where it might be possible to arrange protection.

trad climbing

Trad, or traditional, climbing is widely considered the most ethical way to climb, and it is the style that many climbers aspire to. The style arose in the early days of climbing, in the late 1800s and early 1900s. Pioneers of the style had little protection other than the rope that linked them together, but today's trad climbers use an array of protection devices.

Trad skills

In trad climbing, the skills required of the climber go beyond pure ability. Placing the equipment safely is a vital skill for the ascending climber. Running belays and anchoring devices are arranged during the ascent by the leader using natural features that the rock face offers. The leader carries a range of equipment such as wedge- or hexagon-shaped nuts threaded on wire or tape, camming devices, and slings for threading through holes in the rock. These are removed by the second climber as he or she climbs. The climb is ascended in stages, or pitches, right to the top of the crag, from where the climbers will usually descend by a path or scramble back to the foot of the climb.

Protection on the climb
Modern protection equipment is sophisticated and, if carefully arranged, provides you with a high level of safety.

WATCH IT
see DVD chapter 1

sport climbing

Sport climbing is a very popular style of climbing that does not require you to use lots of equipment, because all protection is permanently fixed in the rock face.

Climbs are generally a single pitch in length, finishing at an anchor point well below the top of the cliff, from where your partner will lower you back down to the ground. Because you clip the rope into permanent bolts (rather than placing your own protection, as you do in trad climbing), sport climbing can be a quick style of climbing.

Sport climbing techniques

Although sport climbing takes place on a variety of rock types, it is most common on limestone, because the drilled bolts allow blank-looking faces, which lack cracks for traditional protection, to be climbed. Steep routes are common, so make sure you are prepared and have enough energy and power for the climb. The extra reassurance that the bolt fixings give can make a sport climb an excellent opportunity to challenge your skills and try out some new techniques.

Reliable fixings
Bolts may reassure the leader because they are often thought to be more reliable than self-placed protection.

What's the equipment?

All protection is fixed in place in the form of drilled bolts or fixings that have a hanger or an eye through which the climber clips a quickdraw. The rope is then clipped in to provide the protection for the leader. At the top of the climb, the leader clips the rope through an anchor, and is lowered back to the ground. Because of this, sport climbs are no longer than half the length of the rope, but beware – many modern sports climbs can be 30 m (100 ft) or more in length, so in some cases you will need a rope 60 m (200 ft) or even 70 m (230 ft) long.

WATCH IT
see DVD chapter 1

bouldering

Bouldering is pure climbing with several attractions. There are many climbers who only boulder, preferring the simplicity of equipment needed and the technical nature of climbing.

Sociable and immensely challenging, boulderers will often tackle problems that are more difficult than those usually attempted on a climb. For the beginner, it's a good way to train for climbing on cliff and crag. You will need little equipment save for a pair of rock shoes, a chalk bag, and a crash mat.

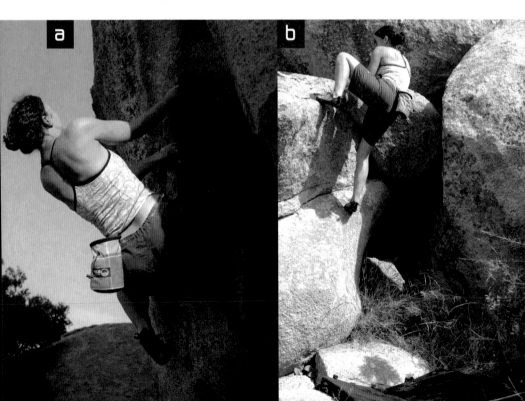

a Safe landing
When you use boulders to learn basic movement, choose a place to climb with a flat, safe landing area at its base.

b Bouldering mats
Bouldering or crash mats are essential and allow you to push yourself to try harder moves much more safely.

c Spotting
Ask a climbing mate to "spot" you (catch or guide you onto your bouldering mat) in case you explode off the rock and land awkwardly if you fail to make the sequence of moves.

d Finding the final holds
You can ask a climbing mate to point out where the crucial finishing holds might be found at the top of the boulder.

c

d

WATCH IT
see DVD chapter 1

getting on to rock

Traditionally, rock climbing was a sub-sport of mountaineering and early climbers had to master both disiplines. Today climbing is a sport in its own right. It takes place not just in the mountains but also on roadside crags, sea cliffs, beaches and, of course, indoors.

a Bouldering venues

Many climbers choose to specialize in bouldering because it gives them the opportunity to practise moves that are more difficult than they might undertake on a climb.

b Indoor climbing walls

Many people who climb in a wealth of locations developed a taste for the sport by beginning indoors. The amenable atmosphere of indoor centres is conducive to rapid progress.

c Sea cliffs

Some of the most exciting places to climb are sea cliffs. Often, accessing the cliffs will be part of the adventure. You may find yourself abseiling down with waves crashing around you or scrambling along the shores of a turquoise sea to reach the start of your climb.

d Mountain crags

Climbing in the mountains is often physically demanding. Parts of the climb may be wet and greasy from water seepage that only dries after weeks of drought. You may also need to climb wearing a backpack containing food, waterproofs, and warm clothing.

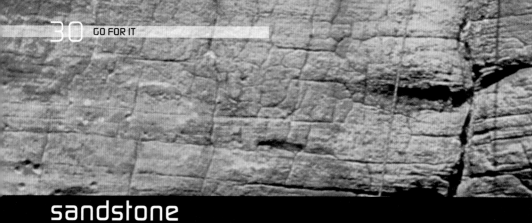

sandstone

Sandstone is found in many parts of the world, but because it is soft and crumbles easily it is only suitable for climbing in certain places.

Where sandstone is relatively soft and eroded, you may only be permitted to "bottom rope" climbs (see pages 120–21). This technique does not require protection devices to be placed in the rock face, which prevents the rock from being damaged. The rope passes through an anchor at the top of the climb, and a belayer safeguards the rope through a belaying device while the climber ascends.

The soft nature of sandstone means that cracks and grooves are common. Features such as overlaps, aretes, and roofs are formed by erosion, and offer excellent holds.

roof

arete

overlap

gritstone

Gritstone is eroded in a similar way to sandstone. It is a much harder rock though, and can be climbed in the trad style.

The most famous gritstone climbing in the world is found in the Peak District, in central England. The area boasts a long tradition of climbing, and climbers there have always been at the forefront of the upward spiral of standards of difficulty.

Gritstone edges tend to be relatively short. Climbs can be led in the trad style from the ground up, placing protection as you ascend. It is also possible to top-rope climbs if you wish – the top of most climbs can also be reached on foot, so it is is relatively straightforward to arrange an anchor point at which the belayer can position themselves safely and securely. A rope is then dropped down to the person climbing up.

Gritstone climbing can be abrasive on hands, legs, and clothing, but it can also be extremely delicate. For some climbers, no other rock type will suffice.

mountain rock

All types of rock described in these pages can be found in the high mountains but one type, igneous rock, is commonly found in the mountains of the UK and in a great many regions of the world.

Igneous rock is formed during active volcanic periods in geological history. It can take many forms, and its characteristics provide some of the most interesting rock on which to climb. Igneous rock, especially rhyolite, offers great features, from cracks to face-climbing on intricate sharp flaky holds, to large roofs, chimneys, and overhangs. Where rock faces have been ground smooth by glacial activity, slabs are often created, which offer superb climbing with a mix of smearing and sharp-edged handholds and footholds.

Because igneous rock is mostly found in mountain areas, routes can be many pitches in length. The profusion of natural features means that placements for protection devices are common, and the durability of the rock means that when securely placed, gear is usually very reliable.

Safe stance
Commodious ledges are often found on mountain rock climbs of lower grades, and provide excellent places for a safe stance.

wall

descent path

slab

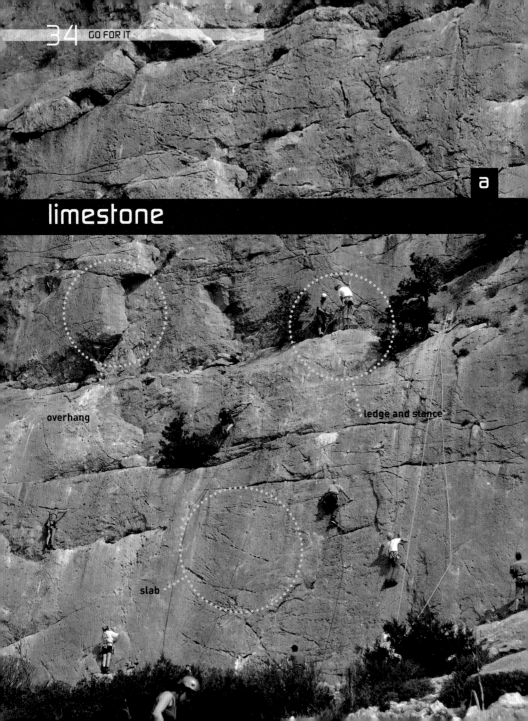

a

limestone

overhang

ledge and stance

slab

Limestone has unique features that climbers enjoy immensely. It can vary from being incredibly compact, smooth, and shiny, to very coarse and rough, with crinkly or razor-edged sharp holds.

In Europe, limestone is one of the most prolific and frequently climbed rock types. It is found high in the mountains and down at sea level, and at all elevations in between. One of the reasons limestone is favoured by climbers is due to the pockets within the rock structure. These can be quite large holes, occasionally large enough to climb into, often with a sharp or pronounced edge to them. At the other end of the scale they can be quite small and you might only squeeze one or two fingers in.

Tufa is a type of rock formation unique to limestone that provides interesting climbs, usually at harder grades. It is formed, in much the same way as stalactites and stalagmites, by water that has run over and through limestone. Tufas take centuries to evolve and are quite rare, but are popular because of the different climbing experience they provide.

Sport climbing
Many limestone crags have become venues for sport climbing (see pages 24–25). Protection is permanently bolted into the rock face.

Limestone pockets
Some handholds require finger strength, more so if the climb is steep.

Climbing on tufa
Many climbers seek out rare tufa formations because they often feature sharp and rounded holds on very steep sections of rock face that might otherwise be unclimbable.

granite

From compact and featureless to rough and intricate, granite comes in many guises. Where it has been subjected to extreme weathering and glaciation it takes on an almost sculptural form. Few finer examples can be found than those in the northern part of Sardinia or on the island of Corsica.

Granite is found in the high Alps of Europe such as Chamonix, on the Cornish coast and in the Scottish Highlands in the UK, and forms the spectacular scenery of the Yosemite National Park and the smooth slabs and walls of Joshua Tree National Park in the USA. Other remote parts of the world that are noted for serious "big-wall climbing" include the southern parts of Greenland and Baffin Island.

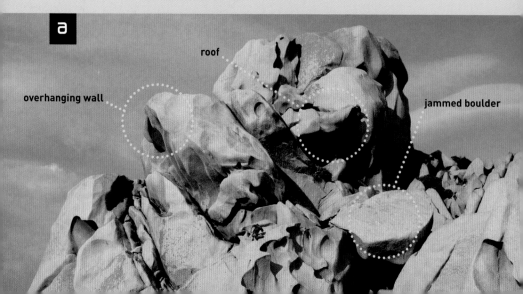

a

overhanging wall

roof

jammed boulder

a Granite crags

Cracks or seams are often a feature of granite crags. You can arrange protection or jam your hands and feet into them (see pages 76–77) to provide a secure enough means of ascent.

b Granite slabs

Although almost entirely devoid of features, granite slabs provide good friction, but they can be very difficult to protect without resorting to drilled-bolt security.

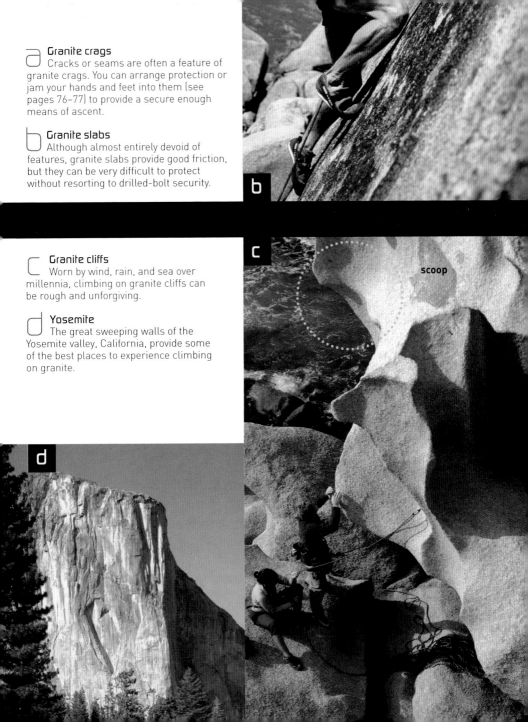

b

c

scoop

c Granite cliffs

Worn by wind, rain, and sea over millennia, climbing on granite cliffs can be rough and unforgiving.

d Yosemite

The great sweeping walls of the Yosemite valley, California, provide some of the best places to experience climbing on granite.

d

go get your kit

coming up...

Safety head-to-toe: 42–47

Investing in good-quality safety gear is vital. From a comfortable, well-fitting harness, helmet, and correct footwear to belay devices and using chalk to improve your grip, here's an overview of the equipment you'll need to safely enjoy your climbs.

Ropes and protection: 48–59

Here, find out about the different lengths and diameters of ropes available and when they are used. Also, learn how to tie the key knots needed in climbing – the figure-of-eight, clove hitch, and bowline. You'll also see the gear required for the rack, from slings to nuts, wires, and karabiners, and understand exactly how this vital equipment system works as a safety chain to hold a fall.

Clothing and bags: 60–65

So how do you know what to wear and carry? This section shows modern-day climbing clothing that provides comfort, style, and protection. You'll also need the right bag to carry your rope, plus a suitable daypack or larger backpack.

the complete outfit

The range of equipment that you will need for climbing, from clothing to safety gear, varies according to the style of climbing and location.

If your first experience of climbing is an indoor climbing wall you may be able to hire footwear and a harness, or borrow kit from a climbing mate. Climbing in the trad style requires slightly more gear – you'll need a harness, climbing shoes, belay device with locking karabiner, a chalk bag, a helmet, and a rack of protection devices.

Clothing
Choose clothing that is comfortable, protects your skin from cuts and grazes, and is suitable for the weather conditions. Go for breathable fabric that will wick sweat away from your body.

Harness
A harness is integral to the safety system. It fits around the waist and legs and the rope is secured to it with a figure-of-eight knot or locking karabiner.

Footwear
Rock-climbing shoes feature smooth, sticky rubber soles. A snug, comfortable fit is essential. Make sure that the shoe does not roll around your foot when you stand on a small hold using the inside or outside edge of the shoe.

Helmet
A helmet is an essential purchase – it protects your head from bangs against the rock face and from falling debris that may otherwise cause serious head injury.

Chalk
Chalk enhances your grip on the rock. However, it also leaves an ugly mark on the rock surface, so always use it sparingly.

Belay device
A belay device is an essential piece of climbing kit. It allows you to hold the rope when a leader or a second falls.

Protection devices
There is a wide range of gear available that can be used to protect the climb. From camming devices and nuts to hexes and slings, each item is designed for use in a different rock feature.

Rope
Different lengths and diameters of rope are used for climbing, and are always classified in metric measurements. 50 m lengths are standard, but longer ropes are also available.

personal safety equipment

Your personal safety is your own responsibility. Make sure you are familiar with the correct way to wear and use safety equipment, such as helmets, harnesses, and belay devices, and always check that they are set up correctly before you start to climb.

All safety equipment used in climbing has to undergo strict testing before it can be sold. The international body that sets these standards is the UIAA (Union Internationale des Associations d'Alpinism). All equipment sold in Europe must feature a CE (European Conformity) mark to show that it has met the required standard for personal protection equipment. Make sure that every item of safety kit you buy has this stamp.

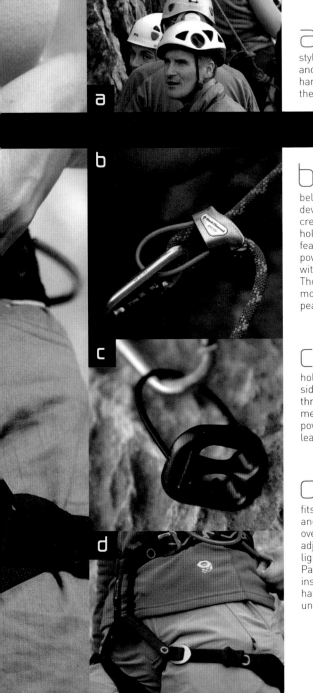

Helmet
There are a variety of helmet styles. All should fit snugly on the head, and some have an internal adjustable harness to hold the helmet away from the head so that air can circulate.

Belay device
With the exception of self-braking belay devices (see pages 88–89), belay devices work by bending the rope to create friction, which increases the holding power (this particular device features a ridged groove to aid holding power). Belay devices are always used with a screwgate locking karabiner. Those with a large rounded end are most suitable and they are known as pear-shaped, or HMS.

Variable-friction belay device
This device offers two levels of holding power depending on which side the controlling rope is threaded through. Many belay devices feature methods of increasing the holding power if you have to stop a falling leader or second.

Harness
Make sure your harness waistband fits correctly on the waist, not the hips, and that the leg loops are snug but not overly tight. Some harnesses have adjustable leg loops so they will fit over light clothing and cold-weather wear. Pay attention to the manufacturer's instructions for safely securing the harness, otherwise it could come undone when you hang in it.

footwear for climbing

Different styles of climbing shoe suit different types of climb and levels of ability. When you have some climbing experience, it will be easier to judge what sort of shoe best suits your climbing style.

Be sure to choose a shoe for your level of ability. Some climbers wear very tight, flexible rock shoes so they can feel the rock surface. This may help where precision is paramount, but it's unnecessary if you are taking your first steps into the sport. Begin with a robust, comfortable shoe. As you develop finesse, and find that you like to feel every nuance in the rock, go for a shoe that is soft and flexible, but fairly tight-fitting.

Some shoes are better suited to certain styles of climbing. Softer shoes can be uncomfortable on multi-pitch climbs, when you're wearing the shoe for several hours at a time. Long routes demand a more comfortable shoe – still snug-fitting, but with some room for expansion. On single-pitch climbs, you might wear the shoes for short spells, taking them off while you rest or belay your partner.

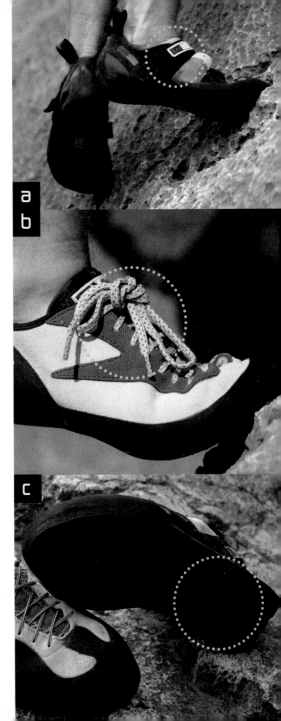

Velcro-fastening shoe
Some of the more technical, flexible shoes are available with velcro fastenings. They are easy to get on and off, but to ensure a snug fit you may have to buy them quite tight-fitting.

Lace-up shoe
Shoe and boot style lace-ups are very popular and most suitable for beginners. They are reasonably flexible along the length of the sole, but have rigidity across the width. This makes it comfortable to stand on the inside or outside edges of the shoe on small holds. When you buy this type of shoe as a beginner, opt for a comfortable fit, rather than an overly tight fit.

Grippy rear sole
Some climbing shoes are designed for all-day comfort and technical climbing, making them more suitable for long, multi-pitch climbs. Some feature a grip pattern on the rear sole, which helps when walking down descent paths.

ropes

Ropes are classified as single or half. When you begin climbing, you'll need only a single rope.

Climbing ropes are made of nylon and perform like low-stretch elastic, absorbing the weight of a fall and protecting the belayer from shockload. This elasticity puts less strain on the safety chain, but the greater the length of rope paid out, the greater the stretch and the longer the fall.

Anatomy of rope
The strength of climbing rope is in the woven core, or kern. The outer sheath (mantel) protects the core from abrasion – this common type of rope is known as kernmantel.

1 Coiling a rope
When not in use, a rope should be coiled or kept loose in a rope bag. To coil the rope, find the middle of the rope and drape it over one hand so it hangs down an arm's length. Lay the rope into your hand, making each loop the same length as the first.

a Single rope
When you start climbing it's best to go for a single rope between 11 mm and 10 mm in diameter as it's more easily held in the hand. The classification of single rope means that it can be used on its own.

b Half rope
For safety, a half rope must be used with a second half rope. Half rope is usually 9 mm in diameter, although 8.5 mm ropes are available. When two half ropes are used, double-rope techniques (see pages 122–23) are required.

c Accessory cord
With a smaller diameter to that of climbing rope, accessory cord is between 3 mm and 8 mm in diameter, and is used for prusik loops, and to hold a nut.

a

2 When you have about 2.5 m (8 ft) left at the end, grip the loops firmly and wrap the end of the rope around the loops. Make three or four turns, working up towards your hand.

3 Form a loop in the end of the rope and pass it through the top of the coils, then thread the end through this loop.

4 Pull the ends through, and the rope is coiled. The ends of rope can be used to tie the rope over your shoulders like a backpack.

tying knots

There are four main knots to learn that are essential for rock climbing (see also pages 52–53).

The principle knot to learn is the figure-of-eight, or tie-on. It is tied in two different ways for different uses. The re-threaded knot is tied through the loops on your harness. Tying a figure-of-eight on a bight of the rope leaves you with a loop you can use to clip into a locking karabiner and attach to your harness (see pages 84–85). Always tie a double-stopper knot after tying a figure-of-eight for safety.

1 Re-threaded figure-of-eight
Tie a figure-of-eight 1 m (3 ft) from the end of the rope, then pass the end through the harness leg loops and waistbelt, as per manufacturer's guidelines.

2 Take the end of rope
and trace it back through the figure-of-eight knot, making sure that all the strands lie flat and snug to each other.

1 Figure-of-eight on the bight
Double the rope over to form a bight (a loop) of about 80 cm (2½ ft). Start the knot by passing the bight under the rope.

2 Pass the bight back
over the double rope, then through the loop that has been formed and pull it tight.

continued >

3 The end of rope should be pointing away from you. Feed through the rope until the loop around the harness tie-on points is about the size of a fist.

4 Tie a double-stopper knot. To start, spiral the end of rope once around the main climbing rope, and then a second time on the figure-of-eight side of the first spiral.

5 To complete the double-stopper knot, thread the end through the two loops that are formed, and tighten it to fit against the figure-of-eight knot.

3 For safety, always finish the knot with a double-stopper knot (see Steps four and five above).

4 The double-stopper knot is an essential safety back-up. Re-tie the knot if you have not left enough rope to tie a double-stopper knot securely.

5 Check that the loop is larger than the diameter of the locking karabiner you will clip it into.

WATCH IT
see DVD chapter 1

Tying knots continued

In addition to the two figure-of-eight knots (see pages 50–51), there are two other essential knots to learn for climbing: the clove hitch and the bowline. You can use the clove hitch to attach yourself to anchor points; the bowline is an alternative knot for tying on to the end of the rope.

1 Clove hitch

The clove hitch is a very quick and easy knot to tie. To begin, form two loops in the rope exactly as shown above.

Bowline

Thread the rope through the harness tie-in points from below. Form a loop in the main rope as shown.

2 Keep hold of the two loops, one in each hand, and pass the righthand loop behind the left.

3 Clip the two loops of rope into a locking karabiner. Remember to screw the sleeve up tight.

4 To adjust the knot to the required length and tension, feed the individual strands through to take up all the slack.

2 Bring the end of the rope through the loop, then pass the end under and around the rope and back in to the loop.

3 Adjust and tighten up the knot by pulling the rope through until a fist-sized loop remains around the harness tie-on points.

4 Tie a double-stopper knot tight against the bowline (see pages 50–51, Steps four and five).

WATCH IT
see DVD chapter 1

the rack

The rack is the name given to the items of safety gear used on a climb. They are carried on your harness gear loops and placed in features in the rock, and the rope is then clipped into them via a quickdraw.

Manufacturers of climbing gear for the rack focus on three key elements: technical features, lightweight designs and materials, and safety.

Camming devices
Cams are crack protection devices which, when placed in an appropriate crack, open out to fit the crack. When subjected to a load the cams are forced to open wider, tightening the device into the crack. You can use cams in parallel and unequal-sided cracks, provided that there is scope for the cams to tighten into the rock.

Nuts
With a wedge-shape design, nuts are arranged in cracks so that when a load is exerted upon them they will tighten into the crack and not pull out. When positioning nuts on your harness gear-loops (known as "racking up"), similar-sized nuts are grouped together and carried on a karabiner. When placing protection, you may be lucky and choose the right-sized nut first time, but having close sizes on the same karabiner means you will find the right size quickly.

Rockcentrics
A rack used for trad climbing (see pages 22–23) will need to have a good selection of rockcentrics (also known as hexes). Depending on the severity of the climb and the protection available, you may need to have more of one size than others. Rockcentrics are designed to be used in tapered cracks but they can also fit parallel-sided cracks. A twisting action will tighten the nut into the crack.

continued >

The rack continued

As well as crack protection devices, you need quickdraws, karabiners, slings, a prusik loop, and a nut key for trad climbing.

Karabiners

There are two basic designs of karabiner – those with solid gates, and wire gates to save weight. You may need to carry 24 or more so saving weight is well worth it.

Quickdraws

Consisting of a karabiner attached to each end of a closed loop, quickdraws are used to clip the rope to protection devices in the rock face.

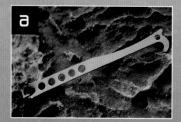

a

b

a Nut key
Use a nut key to retrieve jammed nuts; a double-pronged type can be used to extract cams.

b Prusik loop
Usually made with 6 mm-diameter accessory cord and secured with a double fisherman's (see pages 122–23), this is used as a safety back-up when abseiling.

Screwgate karabiners
A couple of spare screwgate karabiners are useful for tying in to anchors. HMS-style provide more room for the rope.

Slings
Single or double-length slings are used to drape around flakes of rock, to thread around rocks jammed in cracks (chockstones), or through natural holes in the rock.

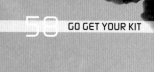

how the system works

To reach the top of the climb or pitch, you must work out the sequence of moves and arrange protection so that if the leader or second falls, they won't hit the ground. Key to this is ensuring that each part of the "safety chain" is understood and implemented.

Leading the first pitch

The leader, the first person to ascend the rock face, has the most precarious position in the team. The second, who climbs next, holds the rope through a belay device and feeds it to the leader as they ascend. The protection devices that the leader places are wedged into cracks in the rock, and the rope is clipped into each one with a quickdraw. If the leader falls he or she should only fall twice the distance from their last piece of protection, because the second locks off the belay device preventing any rope slippage. This system of security, combined with the way in which climbers anchor themselves to the rock, is collectively known as the "safety chain".

Bringing up the second

When the leader reaches the end of the pitch, they secure themselves to an anchor made from the gear that they carry, or to an anchor that is permanently in place. The leader then places the rope through a belay device. Once secured by the leader, the second begins to climb. If the second has difficulty and needs to be held by the rope, the leader is able to keep the rope tight, to prevent a fall of any distance. The second arrives on the belay ledge or stance, makes themselves secure, and the process is repeated until they both reach the top of the climb.

1 The safety chain in action

The leader climbs the first pitch of the route, placing protection where available. The second belays from the ground.

2

The leader falls unexpectedly, but is a short distance above the last piece of gear. The second locks off the belay device and braces himself to hold the fall.

3

The rope tightens and is held in place by the locked-off belay device and each piece of protection. The leader is held on the rope and is unharmed.

WATCH IT
see DVD chapter 1

fair-weather clothing

On hot days you'll want to wear as little as possible as climbing in the heat can be exhausting.

In hot climates many climbers prefer to venture on to rock during the cooler parts of the day, in the early morning or late afternoon and early evening. If you want to climb during the heat of the day you could seek out a crag in the shade, or go to a higher elevation.

Shorts and a vest or T-shirt are comfortable to wear on warm days, although they provide little protection from knocks and grazes, and you risk sunburn. Choose vests or T-shirts made of stretchy, cool fabrics with a high sun protection factor (SPF). If you wear shorts, go for substantial fabric and a sensible design, otherwise you might be left feeling a little vulnerable. Many manufacturers make shorts from specially hard-wearing fabrics that incorporate a stretch element, and these are well worth consideration.

If you want to cover up more, lightweight trousers in a light-reflective colour will prevent sunburn and give you some protection against bumps and scrapes.

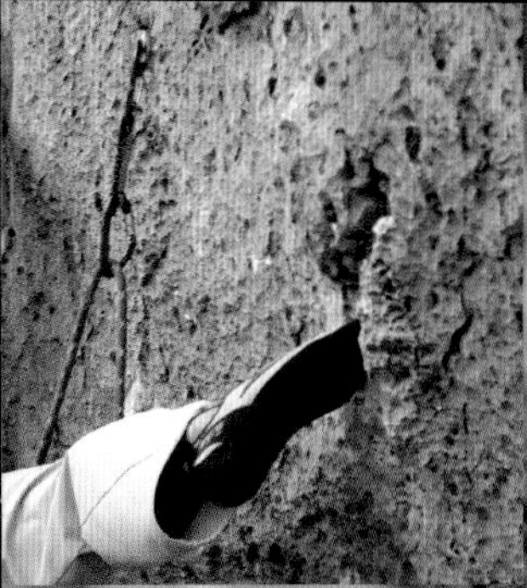

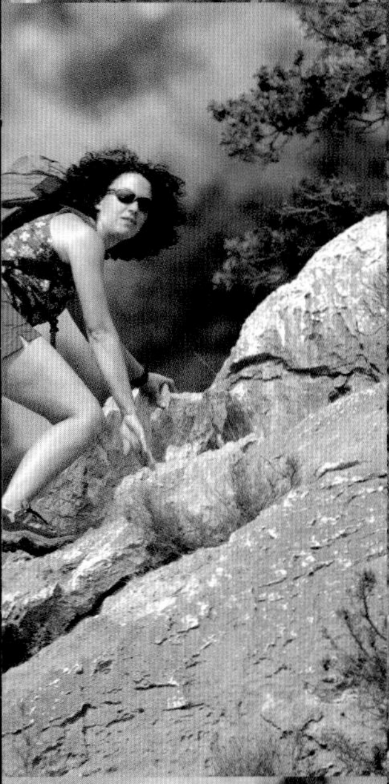

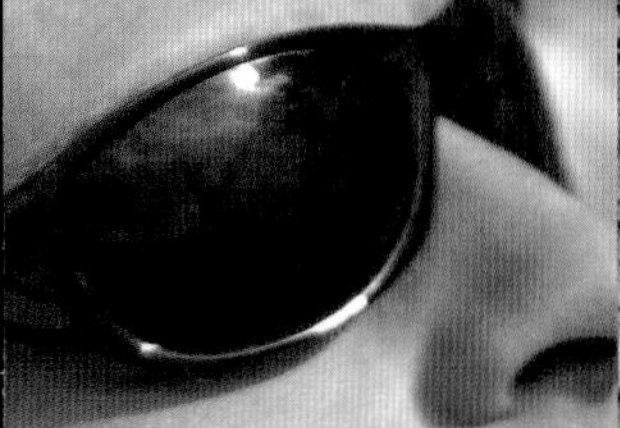

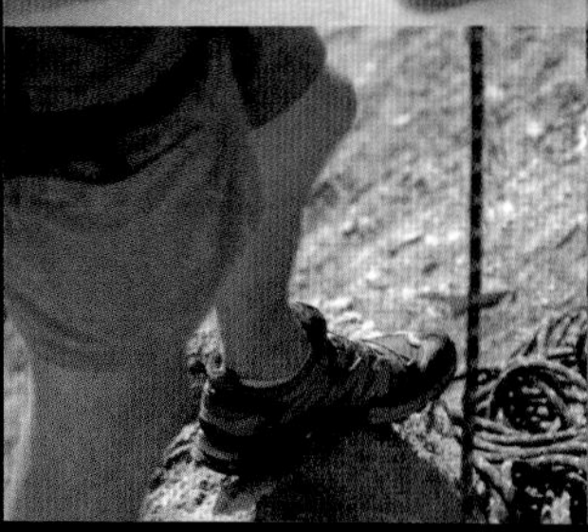

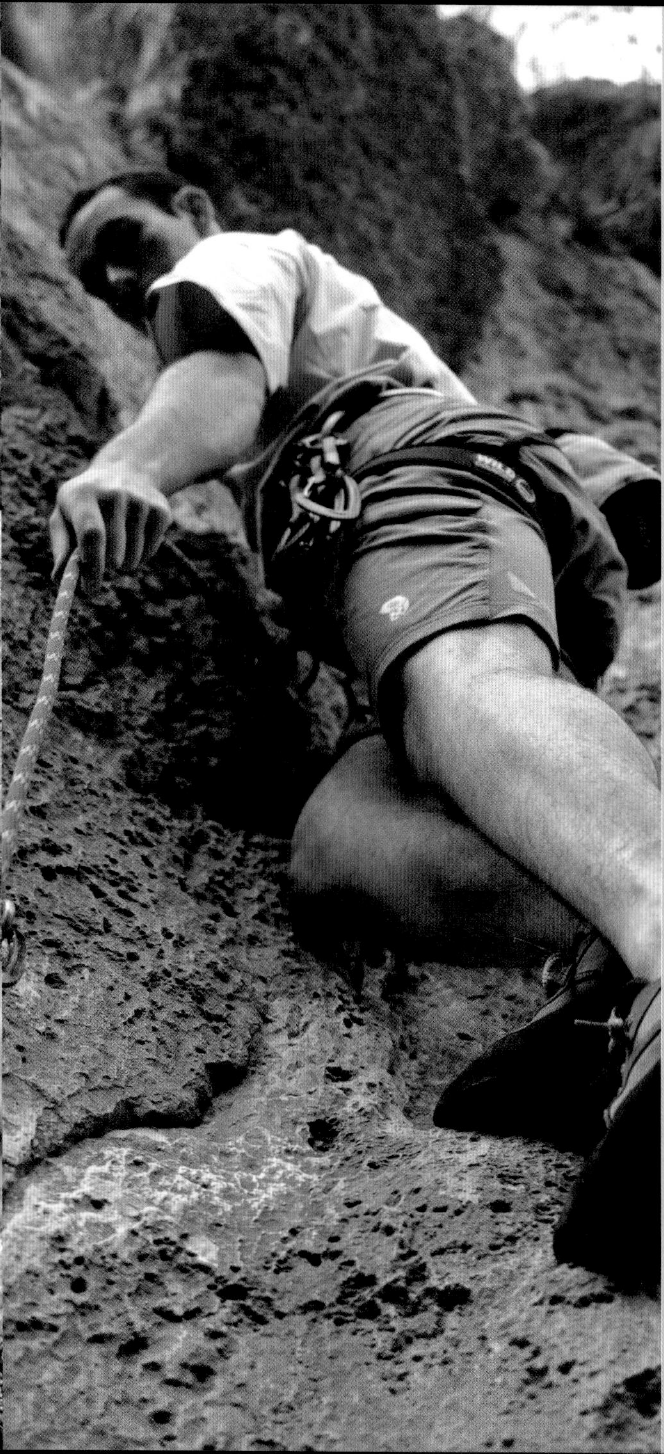

bad-weather clothing

Climbing in heavy rain is unpleasant and the rock becomes incredibly slippery so you will rarely climb in very bad weather, but you may get caught out on occasion. If you go to the mountains to climb, always carry waterproofs and warm clothes.

Layered clothing

You can add layers of clothing to keep yourself warm while you are waiting, or remove layers so you don't overheat on a strenuous ascent.

Base layer

Your base layer should be thermal to keep you warm, and wicking to take moisture away from the skin. Natural merino wool products are far superior to base layers made from synthetic fabrics.

Mid-layer

A fleece makes an ideal thermal mid-layer. You may want two mid-layers if it is extremely cold.

Outer layer

For the outer layer, or shell, choose a waterproof, breathable fabric. In really cold weather, you can wear a down vest or jacket, gloves, and a hat, but you should take gloves off before you begin to climb.

carrying your kit

You'll need a backpack to carry all your kit to the climbing venue. You might also need a backpack for long trad climbs, so that in the case of climbs that finish a long way from their starting point, you can carry spare clothing to wear during the ascent or after the climb. In Europe, backpack capacity is measured in litres.

Staying hydrated

Always take water with you to the crag so that you can stay hydrated during the climb. Water bottles are available in different sizes, as are hydration systems that store water in a plastic bladder that has a tube through which the water is sipped. In some cases these are integrated into a backpack, but can also be bought separately.

Types of water vessel
Water bladders and bottles are a great way of carrying water with you on the climb. If you are undertaking a long climb, choose a vessel that holds around 2 litres (3½ pt) of fluid.

◌ General-purpose bag
A backpack of 30 litres capacity is ideal for carrying clothing and gear to the crag, although a smaller daypack may be used for sport climbing or bouldering. Models are available with a zip closure, or alternatively with an open-top and lid.

◌ Technical-use bag
Some backpacks are specifically designed for rock climbing. A slim design allows the bag to be carried while climbing without impeding arm movements. Loops on the side of the bag can be used to attach items such as ice axes and crampons (for Alpine or winter use).

Using a rope bag
A rope bag is ideal for storing rope and carrying it to the climbing venue. The rope is simply stuffed, rather than coiled, in the bag, which is then carried over the shoulder. Most bags can also be unfolded and layed out to act as a tarp to protect the rope from dust and grit, which can do unseen and long-term damage to a rope.

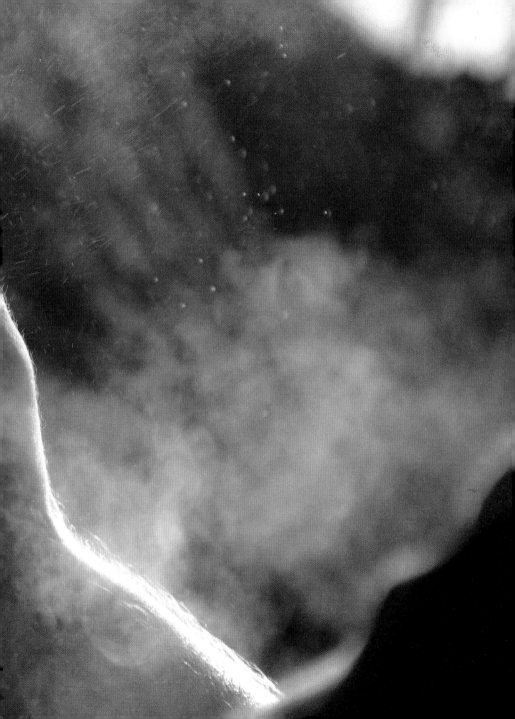

coming up...

Low-level learning: 70–77

Become confident using basic
handholds and footholds to
balance and move over rock
before you attempt long climbs.
If you learn outdoors, or go
bouldering, head for a venue
that is fairly low-angled with
good holds for hands and feet.

More grips and holds: 78–83

When you are confident with the
basics you can progress to more
difficult moves and climbs. A
variety of different types of holds
will help you to learn different
styles of movement over the rock
face. Choose an area of outdoor
rock that is well endowed with
hand and footholds.

Basic rope work: 84–89

Learning the principles of
basic rope work is an essential
part of learning to climb.
Indoor climbing walls are a
great place to take your first
lessons in a safe, secure,
open-all-year environment.

balance and movement

Staying balanced is an important aspect of moving smoothly over rock, and the key to keeping your balance is placing your feet. Learning to trust your rock shoes to stand on smooth rock or tiny protrusions takes time and practice. Your legs have the strongest muscles in your body, so to climb efficiently you must use your feet to their maximum potential.

1 To begin, try moving over a slab of fairly smooth rock by smearing the sole of your rock shoe over the rock and pressing hard to create friction. Use your hands for balance.

2 Climb up and down and across to gain confidence that your feet will stick to the rock. You'll need to make sure the soles of your shoes are clean and dry before setting off.

Efficient climbing

When you need to stand up on a foothold, make sure that you are not too stretched out – many smaller and shorter steps are often more efficient than a big step up. Transfer your weight to the foot that you want to stand up on, and use those powerful thigh muscles to do the work for you. Keep looking down at your feet and judge the most efficient way to move from foothold to foothold.

3 Try to find small ledges or footholds to stand on. You will find it less tiring to stand on the inside or the outside edge of your shoe rather than the toe.

4 Next, mix smearing holds with ledges for the feet, but again use hands only for balance, or the occasional handhold for extra confidence.

WATCH IT
see DVD chapter 2

using handholds

Good footwork is the key to efficient climbing, but you'll also need to use handholds.

Whenever you use a handhold, do so to assist leg and footwork rather than using arm and finger strength alone to pull your body weight up the rock. There will be time enough for this when you graduate to steep or overhanging rock, or climb roofs.

Find a slightly steeper section of rock to practise on. A boulder with a variety of handholds and footholds is ideal. Experiment with pulling on holds both directly downwards and sideways. Try to link a series of handholds together, focussing on maintaining good posture and balance with minimum effort. When you've made a sequence of moves go back to the start of the section to see if you can climb it in a different way. Work out in your mind which is the most efficient route.

Jugs
The best handholds are called jugs. These are big holds that you can curl your hand over, as if you were gripping the rungs of a ladder.

Incut fingerholds
These smaller holds have edges large enough to curl your middle finger joints over.

Fingerholds
You'll need practice and perception to see and use fingerholds, which are any small rock formation you can hold on to. The smaller the fingerhold, the more finesse and technique you'll need to employ to use it to maximum advantage.

Sideways holds
Different sizes of sideways holds can be used to maintain balance during a sequence of moves, or to pull yourself across the rock face.

WATCH IT
see DVD chapter 2

moving over rock

Now you've practised a variety of moves using footholds and handholds, it's time to try a short climb on a rope or tackle a longer boulder problem. The sequence below shows how you might put moves together to progress across a stretch of rock. Before you set off, take a look at the route. Try to spot obvious holds and resting places.

1 The climber starts the climb by placing his hands on a sloping edge, and prepares to move his feet up.

2 Using the sloping edge for the hands, the climber moves his weight up and across on to a high foothold.

3 The left hand is turned to a palming hold allowing him to push his weight over his right foot and reach across rightwards for a hold.

Planning your moves

Before you start, consider the problem from the ground and note where you think the best holds are. Once you set off, keep in mind how you plan to tackle the problem, but don't be afraid to alter that plan if the holds aren't what you expected.

4 He uses the side hold with the palm facing outwards. A resting position is achieved by bringing his left foot up on to the sloping edge.

5 The climber changes his right hand grip to assist the rest and uses his left hand to maintain balance.

6 A high step up and right with the hands essentially in the same position gains the climber a little more height. This means he is able to reach the next handholds.

WATCH IT
see DVD chapter 2

using handholds and footholds

You will use many handholds and footholds and body positions in climbing. Some handholds are used for power pulling, others for balance, and occasionally for pushing. The techniques for using handholds and fingerholds vary according to what the rock has to offer.

Palming
Occasionally the hand can be placed flat against the rock and you can push down on it. In this case the climber is going to move his left foot up. By combining a positive hold with his right hand and pushing down hard on his left he can achieve this more efficiently.

Finger pocket
Just three fingers are used in a finger pocket. The forefinger and ring finger grip the edge of the pocket, while the second finger rests on top of the two. The thumb helps by pulling inwards on a small protrusion. You need good finger strength to pull yourself up on this hold.

Edging

Feet are used on small holds using a technique called edging. It is too tiring to stand on your toes on small ledges with a flexible shoe so instead use the edge of the shoe. Here, the inside edge is used. Using the inside or outside edge depends on where your next move will take you, and how comfortable each feels.

Undercut hold

You can rest on steep rock using an undercut hold – keep your arm extended because it is less tiring. Here a climber is using the hold while he takes off a quickdraw for clipping the next bolt. Using the undercut hold, you can also run your feet up high to make a long reach for a handhold.

High step

Although you should try not to make too many high steps when climbing, it is inevitable from time to time. Having moved your foot to a high hold, transfer your weight directly over it. Push hard on your foot and pull with your hands to complete the move in relative comfort.

c

d

jamming and chimneying

If you are faced with a crack that appears holdless, you can jam your hands and feet in it to progress upwards. If it is a very wide crack, you can get into it and use the sides to lever yourself up, a technique known as chimneying.

Hand jam
Insert your hand into a suitably-sized crack and push your thumb into the palm. Arch your hand to force the fingers onto one side of the crack, and the back of your hand on to the other. Make sure your hand is wedged tightly so the skin can't wrinkle when it takes your weight.

Fist jam
This type of jam is used in wider cracks. Push your fist into the crack and wedge it tight, or make it wider by pushing your thumb into your palm. Keep the skin stretched tight. Fist jams can be used with your palm up or down.

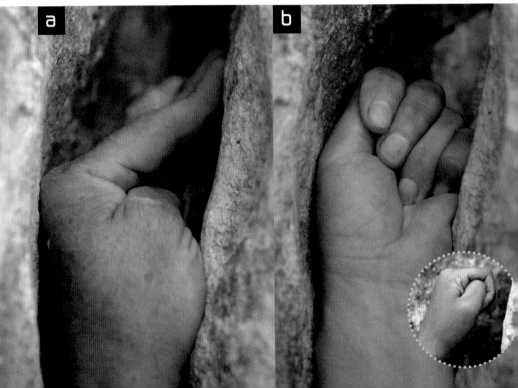

a

b

Chimneying

The most efficient way to climb a large crack, or chimney, is by using a technique known as back and footing. Keep your feet pressed against one side of the chimney and your back pressed into the opposite side. As you step up with one foot, use your arms to push yourself up a little before jamming your legs back across the chimney. If the chimney is wider you will have to straddle across it.

C Finger jam

The finger jam is used in narrow cracks. It's helpful to have a restriction in the crack so you can wedge the lower finger up against it. If you can, get all four fingers in the crack and gain grip by twisting your hand. In extreme finger jams you may have to use one finger.

d Foot jam

Place your foot into the crack and try to twist it in to wedge it tighter. If the crack is wider you may have to wedge your foot lengthways across the crack.

c

d

WATCH IT
see DVD chapter 3

mantleshelfing and overhangs

Mantleshelfing is a technique used to gain a flat ledge where there are no positive holds above. It is very strenuous and requires a certain amount of flexibility and co-ordination to carry out efficiently. Overhangs may have positive holds above them, but climbing them is similarly strenuous. Overhangs can range from a clean-cut outward step in the rock face of just a finger's width, to a much larger feature.

1 Mantleshelfing
Before you start look for some footholds that will enable you to get your feet as high as possible. Reach up with your hands and pull yourself up.

2 When the ledge is at chest height, push yourself up with your feet so you can shift your weight over the top of your hands.

3 Once your hands are flat on the ledge you need to muster some strength and push on your arms until they are straight. This is where the high footholds you spotted are most useful.

Climbing overhangs

You need strength and commitment to climb an overhang. Use an undercut hold while you make a long reach over the lip of an overhang (right), or cut your feet loose then pull yourself over using a jug or bucket handhold (far right).

4 Keeping your arms straight, use your agility and try to get your foot up by the side of your hands. Finding good footholds will help you enormously.

5 With your foot on the ledge push really hard to straighten up until you can bring the other foot up on to the ledge and stand up.

The belly roll
If you fail to straighten your arms in Step 3, you may have to resort to transferring your weight as you would in the standard technique, but then kicking with your leg to lift it onto the ledge, before performing a belly roll.

WATCH IT
see DVD chapter 3

laybacking and bridging

Laybacking is a powerful sequence of moves where the hands and feet work in opposition to each other – pull sideways on your hands, and push away with your feet. Bridging, by contrast, is much less strenuous.

If you lose your footing or hand grip while laybacking, you'll explode away from the rock, so it's worth seeking out a boulder problem or two to practise this technique before using it on a climb. You can bridge across a corner or groove in the climb using footholds on opposite walls or even just by smearing your feet and hands on the rock.

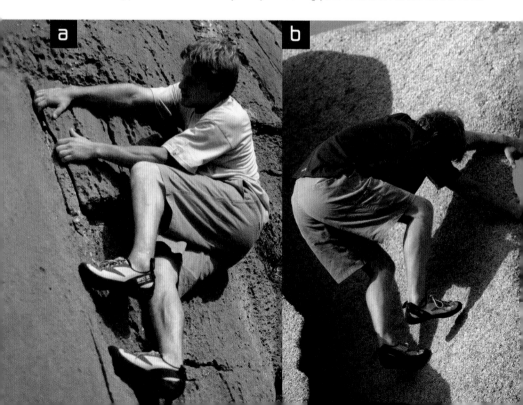

Laybacking

Occasionally, a single laybacking move might help you to overcome a problematical section of the rock face. Remember to keep the pressure on, and only move your feet and hands a little at a time.

Long laybacking sections of climbing are tiring, and it is difficult to hang on and place protection on the lead – do not underestimate the commitment required.

Bridging

This is a great technique to learn to achieve a no-hands rest. Here, the climber has found a comfortable position by straddling a shallow corner and has found a way to drop both hands to the sides for a rest.

Here, the climber is on an overhanging section of rock. He has been able to make a very wide bridge across to a slab to take a good deal of strain off his arms. Both hands are used in a pinch grip to maintain balance.

c

d

WATCH IT
see DVD chapter 3

tying on

Common knots for attaching the rope to your harness are the re-threaded figure-of-eight or bowline (see pages 50–53). An alternative is to clip a figure-of-eight on the bight to your harness with a screwgate karabiner.

a Re-threaded figure-of-eight

Tie a figure-of-eight in the rope and thread the end of the rope through the waistbelt and leg-loop tie-in points (refer to the manufacturer's instructions). Using the end of the rope, re-thread the figure-of-eight. For safety, tie a double-stopper knot with the end and adjust it so that it is tight against the figure-of-eight. Leave a tail of 3 cm (1¼ in) or more otherwise the knot may unravel under load.

b Figure-of-eight on a bight attached to a screwgate

Tie a double figure-of-eight in the end of the rope, ensuring that the finished loop is just large enough to clip into the screwgate karabiner. Clip the karabiner into the harness belay loop and ensure that it is screwed tight. The advantage of this method of tying on to the rope is that it is quicker to swap the rope end from climber to climber.

Tying on tips

- The loop formed on completion of the knot should be just large enough to squeeze your fist through. This loop is a key feature of some belaying techniques (see pages 86–87).

- The knot must be neat and recognizable. All strands of the rope should fit snugly and be symmetrical.

- Always pull the knot tight after tying it – there should be no slack rope through the knot.

- Before you set off on a climb, check again that your harness is buckled correctly and that your knot is tied properly through the right parts of the harness.

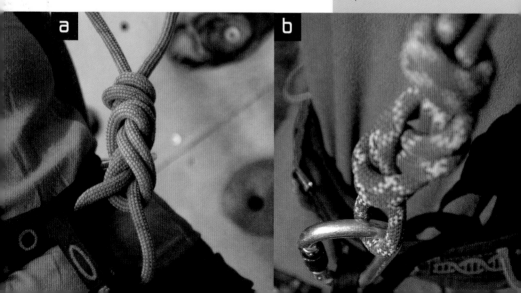

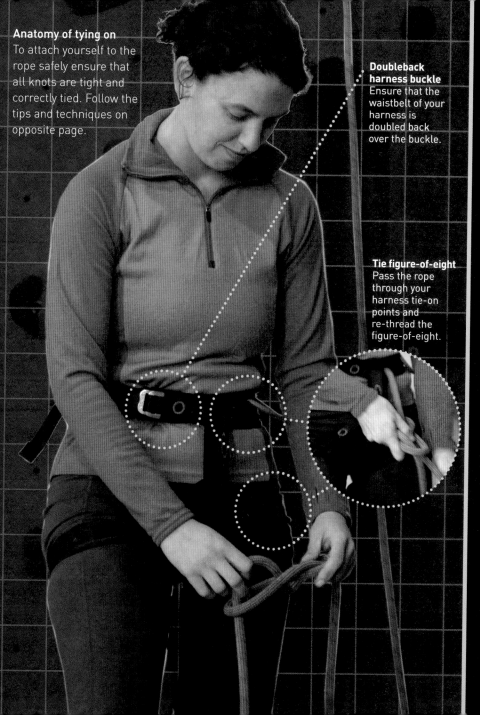

Anatomy of tying on
To attach yourself to the rope safely ensure that all knots are tight and correctly tied. Follow the tips and techniques on opposite page.

Doubleback harness buckle
Ensure that the waistbelt of your harness is doubled back over the buckle.

Tie figure-of-eight
Pass the rope through your harness tie-on points and re-thread the figure-of-eight.

belaying

Belaying is the technique used to hold the rope securely to safeguard your partner on the climb. All belay devices work on the same principle – friction is created by running the rope through the device and around a screwgate karabiner, which is attached to the belay loop of your harness. Holding power is created by locking off the controlling, or "dead", rope by pulling it at a sharp angle away from the loading direction.

Belaying techniques

The technique for belaying differs according to your situation. If belaying a climber who is leading, pay the rope out to the leader as they ascend the route, returning the dead rope to the locked off position when they are stationary.

When belaying a climber from above, such as from the top of the first pitch of a climb, or when bottom-roping (see right), keep the rope tight at all times, with your controlling hand maintaining a constant grip on the dead rope.

Occasionally your partner might need a tighter rope, calling out "tight rope". Pull the rope as hard as you can, maintaining a locked-off position. Sitting back on the rope with the belay device locked off is the best way to get the rope really tight.

1 Belaying when bottom-roping

Grip the live rope with your left hand. Pull it down and use your controlling hand (in this case the right hand) to pull the dead rope through the belay device.

Threading the rope

Take a bight of rope and pass it through one of the holes in your belay device. Ensure the "live" rope passes from the top of the device, with the "dead" rope passing out of the bottom. Clip both the bight of rope and the plastic loop of the belay device through your screwgate karabiner, which should already be clipped to the belay loop on your harness.

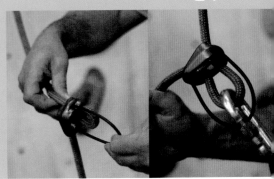

2 As you pull the dead rope through the belay device, simultaneously move your controlling hand down towards your thigh, which places the dead rope at a sharp angle to the loading direction. This is known as the locked-off position.

3 With your left hand, grip the dead rope in the locked-off position while you move your controlling hand back towards the belay device. Grip the dead rope with your controlling hand, then return your left hand to the same position as in Step 1.

WATCH IT
see DVD chapter 4

lowering

The technique for lowering your partner down the climbing wall or crag is the same whether done from above or from below.

Using a belay device
When using a belay device for lowering, the key point to remember is to always hold the rope in the locked off position (see pages 86–87). When lowering from below (right), as in sport climbing or at an indoor wall, you will have the added advantage of friction around the lowering point to assist you to hold your partner's weight.

1 Using a self-braking belay device
A self-braking belay device such as a grigri is useful for sport climbing, but can only be used for lowering from below.

2 Pull the lever back gently until you feel the rope begin to slide slowly through the device, and feed the rope through with your other hand.

3 Make sure that you never lower using the lever alone – keep your other hand on the rope at all times. To stop, let go of the lever and the rope will lock.

Anatomy of lowering from above

When you lower from above, the weight of your partner will be directly on your body, so make sure you are tight to your anchor point and the anchor can take some of the strain. Take the rope in tight and encourage your partner to gradually put their weight on the rope. Hold them for a moment and then run the rope smoothly through the device by gently releasing the rope from the lock-off position – the ideal speed is a slow walking pace.

Lock off the rope

Make sure that you hold the rope in the locked-off position at all times when lowering your partner.

Maintain eye-contact

Being lowered can be unnerving at first, so be sympathetic and maintain eye-contact.

90°

Lean back

Your partner should lean back so that their legs are at roughly 90° to the rock face and their feet are flat on the rock.

WATCH IT
see DVD chapter 4

what not to do

Ropework errors are rare, but to be expected from time-to-time, particularly on early forays to the crag. Take time to think everything through carefully and try to develop a routine for getting organised at the start of the climb. Just before you begin your ascent be sure to have a final check of all knots, buckles, and screwgates – better to discover a mistake at the beginning rather than part-way up a climb.

a Rope tied incorrectly
When you tie on make sure that you follow the manufacturer's instructions for where you thread the rope. Here the rope is threaded through only the leg loop.

b Screwgate not shut
If you forget to screw the sleeve up on a screwgate karabiner the gate might open and the rope detach itself.

c Belaying out of line
Being out of line of the direction of pull may swing you violently to one side and you might let go of the rope in order to steady yourself rather than protect your partner.

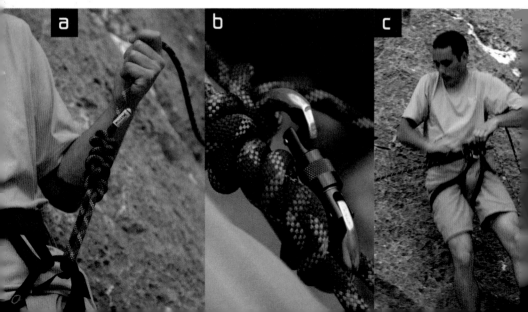

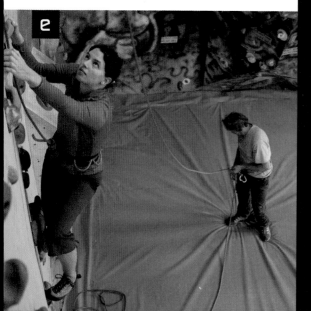

d Frayed rope

Take care to prevent your rope from running over sharp edges, as this can cut through the outer sheath of the rope and damage it so that it must be discarded. Place a sheet or rope bag under the rope to prevent it from becoming abraided when it's on the ground.

e Belaying away from foot of the climb

Standing too far away from the bottom of the climb and not paying attention to your partner can lead to disaster. Always move in towards the bottom of the climb.

Ropework checklist

It is important to ensure you are competent at ropework. Before you start to climb, check that you haven't made one of these common mistakes:

- Not threading the end of the rope through the correct parts of the harness.

- Not screwing the locking mechanism up tight on a screwgate karabiner.

- Positioning yourself out of line of the direction of pull when belaying.

- Not being tight to your anchor.

- Standing too far away from the bottom of the crag or climbing wall when belaying a leader.

- Letting go of the controlling rope when belaying or lowering.

WATCH IT
see DVD chapter 4

coming up...

guidebooks and grading

Guidebooks contain pictures and topographic diagrams of popular crags and cliffs, with the lines of ascent indicated to show you different routes. There are several grading systems in use around the world, each designed to tell you how hard the route is so that you can select a climb within your ability.

Using a guidebook

A topographic diagram is an artwork showing climbing routes. To read one, pick out key features on the crag and relate them to the routes on the diagram. A few prominent features, such as trees or boulders at the foot of the crag, may help to identify start points. Photographs overprinted with lines of ascent are also used in some guidebooks. They can be more accurate than topographic diagrams, but the crag may be foreshortened due to the angle of the shot, making it hard to see where the route goes.

Naming and grading a climb

Those who make the first ascent of a climb have the right to name it and grade it according to technical difficulty and the seriousness of the undertaking. Often, the grading of a climb will change as more people climb the route and gradually reach a consensus as to its difficulty.

The grading system allows you to choose climbs that suit your experience and ability. When venturing onto the rock for the first time, stick to easier grades until you gain more experience in climbing and handling all the equipment associated with the safety chain (see pages 42–43).

Grading comparisons

This table gives you the comparable grading systems in different countries. Grades are always the subject of a great deal of discussion amongst climbers.

Route Grades

British Trad Grade (for bold routes)	Sport Grade	UIAA	USA	AUS
Mod Moderate	1	I	5.1	4
Diff Difficult	2	II	5.2	6
VDiff Very Difficult	2+	III	5.3	
	3-	III+	5.4	8
HVD Hard Very Difficult	3	IV	5.5	10
Sev Severe / HS Hard Severe 3c BOLD / 4a SAFE	3+	IV+ / V-	5.6	12
VS Very Severe 4b BOLD / 5a SAFE	4	V	5.7	14
	4+	V+	5.8	
HVS Hard Very Severe 4c BOLD / 5b SAFE	5	VI-	5.9	16
E1 5b BOLD / 5c SAFE	5+	VI	5.10a	18
E2 5b BOLD / 6a SAFE	6a	VI+	5.10b	19
	6a+	VII-	5.10c	
E3 5b BOLD / 6a SAFE	6b	VII	5.10d	20
	6b+	VII+	5.11a	21
E4 6a BOLD / 6b SAFE	6c	VIII-	5.11b	22
	6c+		5.11c	
E5 6b BOLD / 6c SAFE	7a	VIII	5.11d	23
	7a+	VIII+	5.12a	24
E6 6b BOLD / 6c SAFE	7b	IX-	5.12b	25
	7b+		5.12c	26
E7 6c BOLD / 7a SAFE	7c	IX	5.12d	27
	7c+	IX+	5.13a	28
E8 7a BOLD / 7a SAFE	8a		5.13b	29
	8a+	X-	5.13c	30
E9 7a BOLD / 7a SAFE	8b	X	5.13d	31
	8b+	X+	5.14a	32
E10 7b BOLD / 7b SAFE	8c	XI-	5.14b	33
	8c+	XI	5.14c	34
	9a		5.14d	35
	9a+	XI+	5.15a	36

racking up

Trad climbing demands that you carry a lot of kit, whereas sport climbing is relatively simple, and requires less equipment. As you gain experience you'll develop your own way to rack your gear, but until then, here's how to begin.

Racking up for sport climbing

For sport climbing, you will only need quickdraws and a screwgate karabiner. They are ideally split evenly on each side with all gates facing the same way so that you can release them without having to look down. Some climbers carry a sling with them on sport climbs, and for convenience you could tie it up and clip it to the back of the harness rather than keeping it around your shoulders.

Racking up for trad climing

Your rack is clipped to gear loops on your harness in a structured order so that you don't fumble when finding and removing pieces. Group similar items in order of size so that you can find the right one more easily.

⌐ Nuts
Group nuts of a similar size together. Attach the wires of each group to one karabiner and clip it on to the gear loop. Rockcentric nuts are also grouped by size and carried in the same way as nuts on wire for easy deployment.

⌐ Camming devices
Use individual karabiners to carry camming devices separately because each one will cover a wide range of crack sizes.

⌐ Quickdraws
Split your quickdraws into two groups and attach them on each side of your body, at the front of the harness. You will use them to attach the rope to wired nuts when you place them as running belays.

⌐ Belay device
Your belay device, as well as a nut key and any spare screwgate karabiners, are kept separately from the rest of the rack (often at the back of your harness) because you use them less frequently.

⌐ Slings
Carry your slings looped diagonally over your shoulder. This method makes them easier to detach from your body with only one hand free.

⌐ Chalk bag
Loop your chalk bag to a belt around your waist so that it can slide from side to side for easy access.

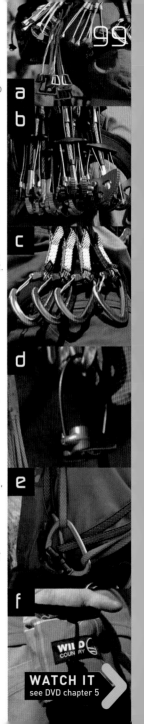

99

a

b

c

d

e

f

WATCH IT
see DVD chapter 5

leading the first pitch

You've racked up and tied on to the ends of the rope, the second is in a safe and comfortable position from which to belay, and you're ready to go! To protect the route as you climb, you need to place appropriate items of gear in the rockface safely and securely (see pages 102–05), and clip your rope to them with a quickdraw.

Before you set off, look at the climb ahead and work out where your first piece of protection will go. Try to place a sound running belay within range of your height. Ideally, place the next piece when your feet are level with the first piece. Thereafter, place runners when you need them, or when the rock allows you to. Get plenty of gear in as you ascend – it's safer.

1 **Using a quickdraw**
There are a number of ways to clip the rope into a quickdraw, but the most reliable method is to loop the rope over the middle two fingers and over your thumb.

2 Use your thumb and forefinger to grip the karabiner and allow the rope to slide off your fingers onto the gate of the karabiner.

3 The rope opens the gate of the karabiner and falls into place. As with most techniques you will find you develop your own style as you gain experience.

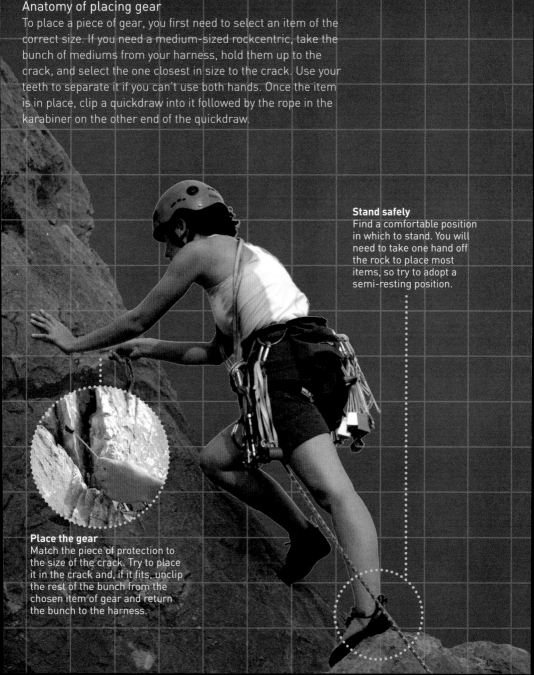

Anatomy of placing gear
To place a piece of gear, you first need to select an item of the correct size. If you need a medium-sized rockcentric, take the bunch of mediums from your harness, hold them up to the crack, and select the one closest in size to the crack. Use your teeth to separate it if you can't use both hands. Once the item is in place, clip a quickdraw into it followed by the rope in the karabiner on the other end of the quickdraw.

Stand safely
Find a comfortable position in which to stand. You will need to take one hand off the rock to place most items, so try to adopt a semi-resting position.

Place the gear
Match the piece of protection to the size of the crack. Try to place it in the crack and, if it fits, unclip the rest of the bunch from the chosen item of gear and return the bunch to the harness.

placing nuts and cams

You'll need a great deal of experience before you can be confident that the protection equipment you place will do the job intended. It's worth practising at ground level before having to hang on with one hand precariously while you attempt to place a crucial piece of gear.

a Good nut placement
Wedge-shaped nuts need to be placed in wedge shaped cracks. The key thing to remember when placing the nut is to make sure that there is plenty of scope for the nut to tighten into the crack when subjected to a loading, ideally above a constriction so that it will not pull through.

b Bad nut placement
If a crack tapers only slightly, or the faces of the nut cannot make full contact with rock, or if the nut is placed too close to the outside of a crack, it may not hold your weight.

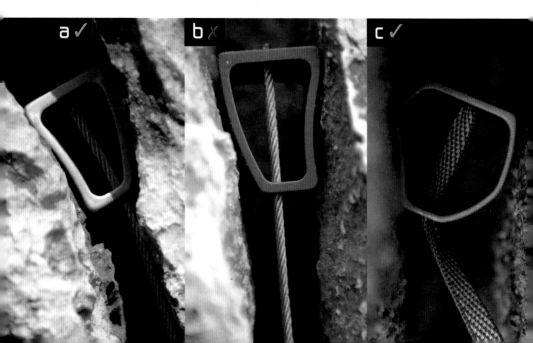

a ✓   b ✗   c ✓

Good hex placement
Hexagon-shaped nuts, or hexes, can be used in much the same way as wedge-shaped nuts. They have an advantage because they can be used in roughly parallel-sided cracks. The twisting action that a load places on a hex tightens it against the walls of a crack.

Bad hex placement
It is essential to choose the hex that fits snugly into a crack, and make sure the faces have good contact with the rock. Otherwise it will twist out of the crack under load, rather than tightening into it.

Good cam placement
The perfect placement for a camming device is where each of the four cams is in contact with the rock. This gives plenty of scope for the cams to bite under load. To place a cam, you squeeze the trigger so it closes, place it in the crack, and release the trigger gradually until all the cams bite.

Bad cam placement
If the cams are quite wide open, or one or more fails to make contact with the rock at all, it is unlikely to hold. Another common mistake when placing a cam is to place it with the cams entirely closed – it will hold, but will be almost impossible to remove.

d ✗

e ✓

f ✗

WATCH IT
see DVD chapter 5

placing slings and quickdraws

When creating protection, slings are used in two main ways – threaded or looped. Other items of gear may need to be extended with a quickdraw. The second may need to use a nut key to dislodge tightly-wedged gear.

a Sling looped over a flake

You can drape a sling over a small flake of rock. If the flake is shallow, the loading must remain well below it for it to be an effective anchor point. It is very important when looping slings over blocks or flakes in this way that you do not place the sling too tightly around the rock. Doing so weakens the sling quite dramatically.

b Threaded sling

A sling threaded through holes in the rock is called a "thread". Rock edges can be very sharp and may cut through a sling if a load is exerted upon it. Only use a threaded sling if you are confident the rock is smooth enough.

c Placing quickdraws

Quickdraws are used to extend runners attached to gear placed in cracks to prevent the action of the rope running through the

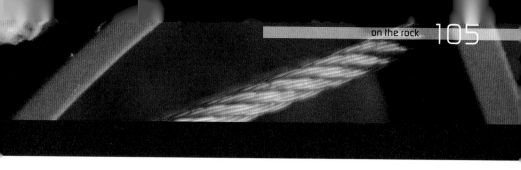

karabiner from lifting the gear out. One end of the quickdraw is clipped into the runner, and the other into the rope. Try to make sure that the gate of the karabiner into which you clip the climbing rope is facing away from your direction of travel.

d When to use quickdraws
Wire runners, most often found on wedge-shaped nuts, should always be extended. The tape runners used with cams and hexes rarely need extending because they have more flexibility to absorb the pull of the rope. However, as shown below, sometimes there is a clear case for extending a tape runner with a quickdraw.

e Removing gear
Very occasionally, you may have difficulty removing gear from the rock. It may be seated very securely, or it may have worked loose and fallen deeper into the crack. A nut that has been fallen on by a leader will be extremely difficult to remove.

f Using a nut key
To remove gear that is stuck fast you can use a nut key. There is no particular technique for doing so – it depends on how the gear is wedged. Quite often a solid push on the nut from below will be sufficient to dislodge it from its placement. Sometimes, you might find that hooking it from above works better.

WATCH IT
see DVD chapter 5

taking in

Once you have reached the top of the first pitch and are comfortable and safe on the stance (see pages 108–11), it's time to bring up your partner. You will need to use climbing calls to communicate with your partner throughout the process of taking in the slack rope and belaying your second.

Belaying from above

Check that you are secure to your anchors, take in the the rope, thread it through the belay device, and attach it to the tie-in loop on your harness with a screwgate karabiner. Always set up the belay device so that the controlling rope is on the same side as the ropes that link you to the anchor. Check that you have plenty of unrestricted space to operate the device. Here's a quick reminder about how to belay – for the full instructions see pages 86–87.

1 Pull the live rope up and through the belay device with your controlling hand. Remember that throughout the process, your controlling hand can only be used to grip the controlling rope. The other hand can be used to grip either.

2 Move the rope into the locked-off position, then take your left hand off the live rope and place it on the dead rope close to the belay device.

3 Place the controlling hand between your left hand and the belay device, then go back to Step 1 and repeat the process.

Climbing calls at the stance

Climbers use a series of recognised calls
to communicate during the various stages
of the climb. These are kept deliberately
succinct to avoid confusion. As you gain
experience, you may develop your own
system, but here is a sample sequence of
calls that climbers might use when the
leader reaches a stance:

- **"Safe"**: leader has arrived at the top of the
  climb, or at a stance part-way up a climb,
  and has made themself safe.
- **"Take in"**: second has taken the rope out
  of the belay device and is ready for the
  leader to take in the slack rope.
- **"Taking in"**: leader is taking in the slack
  rope between the two climbers.
- **"That's me"**: second calls out that the
  rope is tight between the two climbers.
- **"Climb when ready"**: leader has second
  on belay and is ready for them to climb.
- **"Climbing"**: second has started to climb.
- **"OK"**: leader is ready to hold the second.

Climbing calls during the climb

The following calls are used whilst each
of the climbers is actually climbing, rather
than at stances and belays:

- **"Watch me"**: climber is in difficulty and
  fears they might fall.
- **"Tight rope"**: second is in difficulty and
  wants to be held on the rope.
- **"Take in"**: climber asks belayer to take
  in excess slack rope.
- **"Slack"**: climber asks belayer for more
  rope to clip a quickdraw above the head
  or to climb more quickly.

using a single anchor point

When you arrive at the end of the pitch, you'll need to make yourself secure to the rock so that you can bring up the second. You can use a sling threaded around a tree or a solid flake, or through a hole in the rock. Occasionally you may find a permanent (in situ) piece of gear that you can use as an anchor point.

Creating a safe stance

A single anchor point is the simplest to rig. Here are three ways to attach yourself to the anchor:

a Sling clipped to harness
If the distance from the anchor point to a comfortable place to sit or stand is the same as the length of the sling, clip it directly to the rope loop of your harness. Use a screwgate karabiner, and lock the gate tight.

b Clove hitch tied to harness
If you need to be further away, clip the rope into the anchor point with a screwgate karabiner, screw the lock tight and, while holding the rope, move into your preferred position. To secure yourself, put a large pear or HMS screwgate karabiner through the tie-in loop (see detail), and use a clove hitch (see pages 52–53) to secure the rope. Lock the karabiner tight and then adjust the clove hitch so that the rope back to the anchor is snug.

c Clove hitch tied to anchor
If your anchor point is within arm's reach of where you will stand to belay, tie a clove hitch directly to the anchor via a screwgate karabiner.

a

b

c

WATCH IT
see DVD chapter 5

using multiple anchor points

If you have to construct an anchor from nuts or cams, it is advisable to use more than one placement. This is known as using multiple anchors.

Creating a safe stance with multiple anchors

The same principles of gear placement, positioning, and fastening apply to multiple anchors as to single anchors. Always use screwgate karabiners, or two karabiners arranged with their gates back-to-back, to attach yourself to anchor points. Here are three methods of using multiple anchors, but there are lots more combinations.

a Clove hitch tied to harness
Clip the rope into one anchor and bring it back to an HMS karabiner attached to the tie-in loop. Secure it with a clove hitch (see pages 52–53). Repeat the process for the second anchor. You can adjust the clove hitches so that the tension on each anchor is even, and any load is divided equally.

b Clove hitch tied to anchor
If you are within arm's reach of the anchor, a quick way to secure yourself to a second or third is to tie the clove hitch directly to the anchor. If you have to move a long way away from the anchor point, consider having another anchor point close by. Attach yourself to this using a clove hitch directly to the anchor.

a

b

C

C Linking anchors with a sling

Two anchors can be linked together with a sling. Tie an overhand knot in the middle of a sling and clip one loop into each anchor. Anticipate which direction the load is likely to come from, and adjust the overhand knot so that when you clip in a screwgate karabiner the load will be divided equally between the two anchors. Clip the screwgate karabiner into each loop on either side of the overhand knot. This is vital – if you don't do this and one anchor fails, there could be a shock loading on the remaining anchor, causing it to fail too. Now attach yourself to the anchor as you would tie in to a single anchor (see pages 102–03).

leading the second pitch

When you are both at the top of the pitch and the second is tied to the anchor, you have some organizing to do. You may decide that the second will become the leader for the next pitch. This is called leading through, or swapping leads. The new leader re-organizes the rack on their harness, checking all equipment is in place, then sets off. If you are not swapping leads, follow the steps below.

1 The belayer takes in the rope as the second climbs up. Here there is little room for two climbers so the second will have to hang from the anchor.

2 Once the second reaches the stance, the belayer keeps them on belay until they have tied into the anchor and are in a comfortable position.

3 With the second tied into the anchor, the belayer takes the rope out of the belay device. From this point on, the belayer and second assume new roles.

Fall factor

The fall factor is the length of the fall divided by the length of the rope paid out. The maximum the system can cope with before failure is a fall factor of 2. Shown far left, the leader is about 3 m (9 ft) above the second, which could result in a fall of 6 m (18 ft): 3 m (9 ft) of rope has been paid out so a fall here would generate a fall factor of 2, and the weight of the leader would fall on the belayer. Shown near left, the leader has placed a new runner. This reduces the fall length to 2 m (6 ft) and so lowers the fall factor to 0.6. It also removes the danger of the leader falling on the belayer.

4 The belayer now becomes the leader so retrieves the rack from the second. The second becomes the belayer and re-arranges the rope so that the leader's end of rope will run smoothly from the top of the pile.

5 When the rope has been run through and the leader has re-arranged the rack, the second has the leader on belay, and the leader is then ready to set off.

6 The leader should try to place a good piece of protection soon after leaving the stance, so that if they fall, the load won't be placed directly onto the second. Placing gear also helps prevent a high fall factor.

WATCH IT
see DVD chapter 5

abseiling

Abseiling is a great way to get down from a climb. A slabby crag about 20 m (65 ft) high is big enough for a first attempt, and if you can easily walk around the side it is ideal. Arrange anchor points at the top of the crag – it helps if they are much higher than the starting off point. Use a safety rope operated by a belayer who ties in to the rope end and attaches to the anchor point. They will hold your weight if for any reason you are unable to cope.

1 The abseil rope can be double or single rope. Double rope will create more friction and give you more control. Halve the rope, tie a figure-of-eight on the bight (see pages 50–51) and clip it to the anchor with a screwgate karabiner. Thread the double rope through and around your figure-of-eight abseil device.

2 Attach the small hole in the abseil device to the belay loop of your harness with a locking karabiner. The safety rope is clipped or tied directly to the harness.

3 The hardest part of any abseil is setting off. Try to keep your weight on the abseil rope and use your harness to pull against the rope. Your speed is controlled by creating extra friction around the figure-of-eight and gripping the rope tightly or loosely.

4 Keep your feet high and legs straight. In this position you can walk backwards at a steady pace down the rock. Do not bound down the rock like you might have seen in the movies – a steady descent in contact with the rock at all times is a safer technique to nurture.

WATCH IT
see DVD chapter 6 >

abseil safety

In order to reach the bottom of the crag and retrieve your rope, you'll need to abseil in stages that are just less than half the length of the rope. If you are climbing on a single rope this can be time-consuming, so climbers tend to descend by abseil only if they are climbing with two ropes. The ropes are joined together with a double-fisherman's knot (see pages 122–23).

Abseiling with a belay device

To set up the rope for abseiling, loop the rope around or through an anchor point so that when you reach the bottom and pull one end, the rope slides smoothly and can be retrieved. Thread both ropes through the belay device and clip both loops into a HMS karabiner attached to your harness belay loop. Screw the locking sleeve up tight. You can now set off, but it's a good idea to use a safety method (see below). Alternatively, ask someone to hold the end of the abseil rope or ropes. If the abseiler gets into difficulty, the second person pulls hard on the ropes and the abseiler will not descend further until the rope is slackened.

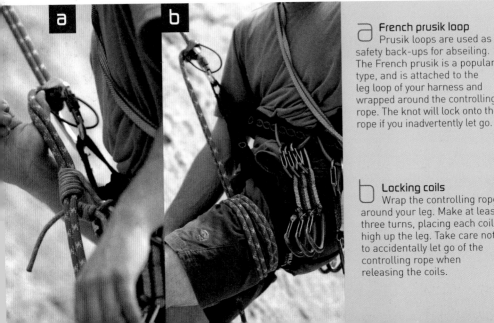

a

b

a French prusik loop
Prusik loops are used as safety back-ups for abseiling. The French prusik is a popular type, and is attached to the leg loop of your harness and wrapped around the controlling rope. The knot will lock onto the rope if you inadvertently let go.

b Locking coils
Wrap the controlling rope around your leg. Make at least three turns, placing each coil high up the leg. Take care not to accidentally let go of the controlling rope when releasing the coils.

Anatomy of abseiling safely

In order to abseil safely, use a back-up device. The French prusik is the simplest device to use. To set it up, clip a screwgate karabiner into the leg loop and clip one end of the prusik loop in with the joining knot up against the karabiner. Spiral the loop around the two abseil ropes for a minimum of four turns. Clip the loop back into the screwgate karabiner and lock it tight.

Avoiding jams
Make sure that no baggy clothing, long hair, or any of your gear (particularly slings) can become entangled in the abseil device. Items jammed in the device can cause serious problems.

Tying the French prusik
Tie the French prusik so that it is not too long. If it butts up against the abseil device when it's under load, it will not lock off efficiently, if at all.

WATCH IT >
see DVD chapter 6

lowering off a sport climb

When you reach the top of a sport climb you will need to be lowered off back to the ground. All sport climbs are equipped with a lower-off anchor, which come in the form of a steel karabiner into which you clip your rope, or more commonly, a sealed ring (known as a "maillon") or a double "eco" bolt as shown here.

Lowering safely
The belayer must be prepared to take the weight of the leader (see right) and adopt a solid stance either sitting down or standing up. Be sure to communicate at each stage of the lowering off process so that each of you knows what is going on.

1 Lowering off
When you reach the anchor, take a quickdraw or sling and attach yourself to the lower-off point. This method is known as a cowstail.

2 Ask your second for slack rope and thread it through the lower off point. Tie a figure-of-eight in the bight (see pages 50–51) and clip it to your belay loop.

3 Now you can untie from the end of the rope. Pull it out of your harness and then pull the end through the lower-off. Check that everything is in place.

4 Instruct your second to take your weight. Pull into the anchor a little and detach your cowstail. Shout down that you're ready to be lowered back to the ground.

Anatomy of lowering off
To lower off safely, attach yourself to the lower-off point with a cowstail, thread the rope through the lower-off points and attach it to your harness, then untie your original knot from the rope.

Clip into the anchor
Use a cowstail to clip into the anchor point. The cowstail is a short sling looped through the harness tie-on point in a "lark's foot" knot.

Thread the rope
In a double eco-bolt lower-off system, first thread the rope up through the bottom bolt, then through the top bolt.

Untie from the rope
Only untie from the end of the rope once you have threaded the rope through the lower-off point and tied a figure-of-eight in the bight, then clipped it to your harness belay loop using a screwgate karabiner.

WATCH IT
see DVD chapter 6

top- and bottom-roping

In a top-rope system climbers are belayed from above, while in a bottom-rope system thay are belayed from below. For both systems, you need to rig anchors at the top of the crag (see pages 108–11). If they are a long way from the edge, use a separate low-stretch or static rope.

Using a top-rope

To use a top-rope system, you need to be able to walk around to the top of the crag and set up an anchor and stance in the same way as if you had led the climb. You then throw down a rope to the person who will climb, then they tie on and climb up to you, belayed from above.

1 Top-roping
The belayer should be positioned close to the edge of the crag, where he or she can look over and see the whole of the climb. Make sure that you are tight to the anchor.

2 Safeguard the climber using a belay device. It is always sensible to try to keep the rope between belayer and climber fairly snug at all times. This instils confidence that the rope will hold the climber if they slip.

3 When the climber reaches the top of the climb, the belayer can lower them back to the bottom of the crag.

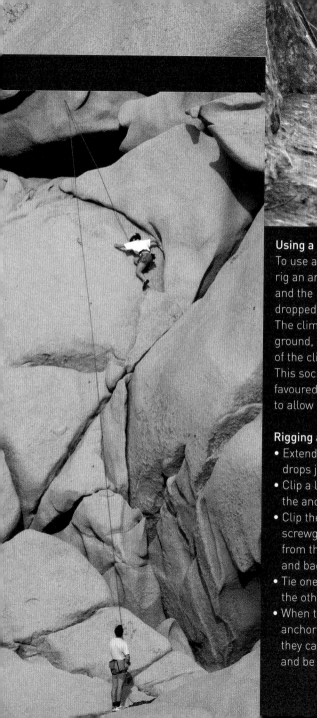

Using a bottom-rope

To use a bottom-rope system you rig an anchor at the top of the climb, and the rope is doubled through and dropped to the bottom of the crag. The climbers are belayed from the ground, and when they reach the top of the climb, are lowered back down. This sociable method of climbing is favoured on short outcrops of rock to allow groups to climb together.

Rigging anchors for bottom-roping

- Extend the anchor tie-in so that it drops just below the top of the crag.
- Clip a large screwgate karabiner into the anchor tie-in.
- Clip the climbing rope into the screwgate karabiner so that it runs from the ground up to the anchor, and back to the ground again.
- Tie one end to the climber and use the other end to belay.
- When the climber reaches the anchor tie-in at the top of the climb, they can put their weight on the rope and be lowered back to the ground.

double-rope techniques

All the roped climbing we have seen so far uses a single rope. Sometimes the route will weave around, linking holds together. You place protection where it's needed, which might mean that the rope zig-zags up the crag, causing massive friction or rope drag – perhaps to the point where it becomes impossible for the leader to move! To solve this problem, climbers use two ropes. These are usually thinner than a single rope – 9 mm instead of 10 or 11 mm.

Clipping ropes alternately
Try to clip each rope into alternate pieces of gear. Sometimes you may need to clip one rope into a sequence of runners so that when you're higher up the pitch, the other rope runs to your second in a straighter line.

Using two ropes
To use double ropes, keep one rope to your left when you make moves to the right, and the other to the right when you make moves to the left.

Using two ropes

The left image shows how to use double ropes on a zig-zagging route, while the right image demonstrates the rope-drag problems caused by using a single rope on the same route. When belaying double ropes, you may need to pay out or take in one rope but not the other – practice will make you proficient. At all times, you must be ready to hold a falling climber.

When tying in to anchor points, the ropes can be split between the anchors (see pages 102–05). You can also make longer abseil descents than with a single rope. Join the ends of each rope together with a double fisherman's knot and then thread them through an anchor point to descend.

1 Tying a double fisherman's Spiral one rope twice around the second rope. The second turn should go back over the first turn.

2 Tuck the rope end through the double loop that is formed.

3 Repeat the process with the second rope working the spirals towards the first knot you tied. The turns go in the opposite direction to the first part of the knot.

4 Slide the two knots together. Each should fit snugly inside the other, and the reverse of the rope should show four strands lying side-by-side.

solving simple problems

There are few things to go wrong in climbing provided that you handle all the ropes and gear with care, think things through carefully, and discipline yourself to be safe at all times. One of the most useful safety measures is to tie off the belay device. This will come in useful when the leader is in difficulty on a climb and needs to hang around on the rope, or if you need two hands to sort out a tangle in the rope when you are lowering someone.

1 Tying off your belay device
Hold the belay rope in the locked off position and thread a loop of the controlling rope through the belay karabiner.

2 Thread a bight of the controlling rope through the first loop and pull it tight to form a hitch, making sure that you have a bight of about 50 cm (20 in) in length.

Locking off the rope

Abseiling can pose problems. If you throw the ropes down the crag, always take care that they don't become tangled, although inevitably, there are times when they will. By using a French prusik knot or locking coils (see pages 116–17), you will be able to let go of the rope, allowing you to use both hands to sort out the tangle.

3 Thread the rope through a second time to make another hitch for extra safety.

4 Now you can release your hands from the rope to do whatever you need to do, or to have a rest from holding a climber.

5 To free the rope, release the second hitch. Then undo the main hitch by tightly gripping the controlling rope at the belay device (to avoid slack rope), and pulling it out of the belay device.

WATCH IT
see DVD chapter 4

go further

coming up...

Improving fitness: 130–35

Stretching exercises are useful for warming up your muscles prior to climbing. There is also a range of climbing techniques you can employ to develop endurance and muscle strength.

Improving technique: 136–43

Strength and stamina become increasingly important attributes as you progress through the grades and desire to climb harder and better.

Climbing horizons: 144–51

There are so many places in the world to climb that it's impossible to list every one. The venues and types of climbing included in this section should give you a great taste of what the vertical world has to offer.

warming up

Some of the moves that you make when climbing use muscles in a way that your body may not be familiar with, so take time to do a few simple stretching exercises before you begin. A lengthy walk to the climb will probably give you enough aerobic exercise to warm up, but it won't stretch your muscles much, particularly shoulders, fingers, and arms. Simple climbing at the foot of the crag will also help you to warm up.

a Finger stretch
Stretch your fingers by holding your arms out in front of you with your palms facing away. With one hand, gently pull back on the outstretched fingers so that you feel a small amount of tension in your forearms. Hold this position for about 15 seconds, then swap arms.

b Tricep stretch
Stretch your triceps by placing your hand behind your head and gently pushing back on the elbow with the other hand. Hold for 15 seconds and repeat with the other arm. Make circles with both arms outstretched first one way and then the other.

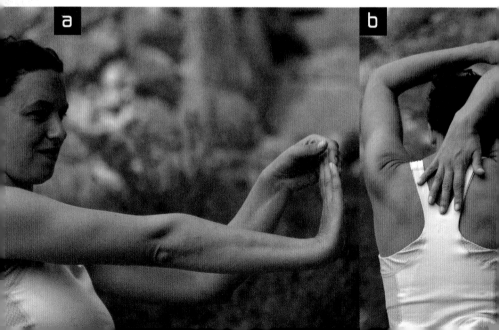

c

Shoulder stretch

Hold your arm out straight at shoulder height and gently pull it across your body. Turn your head to face towards the shoulder, but try to keep your torso still. At the point you feel the stretch, stop and hold for about ten seconds and then slowly release.

Leg stretch

Stand with your feet apart then gently stretch to the side. Hold for about 15 seconds before transferring to the other leg.

Calf stretch

Stand on one leg (you can hold on to something for support) and lift the other behind you. Hold the ankle with one hand, and gently push your hips forward to increase the stretch.

d

e

increasing endurance

Practising on a climbing wall or by bouldering is a good way to develop endurance and strength. Climbs at the wall may only be around 10 m (33 ft) or so in length, so it's possible to climb a number of routes in a few hours with good rests in between. Traversing the wall at about waist height gives sustained periods of exercise that are good for building stamina.

A high level of fitness is an advantage in climbing, but you'll need specific training to increase your endurance. There will be moments when you'll need short bursts of power, followed by sustained, strenuous action. To prepare yourself, choose climbs or problems with longer sequences of moves rather than short, powerful three- or four-move problems.

An important part of increasing endurance is learning to rest. Wherever you can, find places where you can take one or both hands off the rock and dangle them below waist level for a few seconds or more.

Red-pointing a climb

If you are leading a climb on which reaching the top is your priority, rather than the purity of the way you do so, falling off each time you fail to make the moves is acceptable. In the long term, this will help to build stamina so that one day you will be able to climb such difficult routes in one push. Climbing a route in this way is known as "red-pointing".

1

Training on steep rock

Climbing on very steep, overhanging rock is an excellent way of building endurance and learning how to use energy efficiently. To make the ascent without falling or resting, you will need to develop technical climbing skills in addition to strength and endurance.

2

A good tactic for training is to practise a climb on a top- or bottom-rope (see pages 120–21). This allows you to take rests on the rope if you do not have the power to make all the moves in one continuous push. You can also use such a rest to run through the sequence of moves in your mind.

3

Continue the climb after you have had sufficient rest. Being able to work out a series of moves quickly in these situations saves energy.

building muscle strength

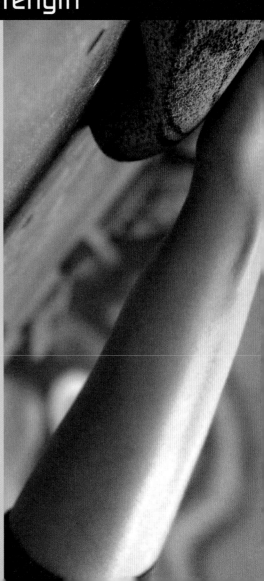

If you want to progress to harder climbing grades you'll need to develop muscle power. There are few things better for doing this than climbing itself. Make sure that you build up muscle strength gradually so that you don't damage tendons or pull muscles, as they will take a long time to heal.

Building finger strength

To build finger strength, climb on slightly overhanging walls with small but very positive holds. It helps to have good footholds that can take much of the strain, and over time you can progress to smaller-size footholds. Vary the type of fingerholds you use to include side-pull holds as well as straight-pull holds.

Building forearm strength

To increase forearm strength, pull on larger holds and on steeper rock with smaller footholds. Again, vary the styles of hold that you use.

a Developing forearm strength
Using large holds for your hands will develop strength in your forearms. Place your feet on large or small footholds, or let them hang free to develop even stronger forearms.

a

b

b Building all-round strength
Varying the holds you use and the type of boulder problems you attempt will develop unique strength. Here the move is awkward and the handholds large but open, requiring an unusual amount of power.

c

c Developing finger strength
An overhanging wall on small holds demands finger strength. Practise using small positive finger holds, but always warm up before pulling on anything too tiny.

d

d Varying training
To build the best possible all-round strength and technique, keep your training as varied as possible and try to replicate the moves you will find on a climb.

climbing competitively

Competition climbing has become an important part of the climbing world, with competitors frequently pushing the limits of technical difficulty. It is also a great way to improve your climbing skills. A range of events exists that are open to new climbers as well as experienced ones – your local climbing wall may run competitions that are open to all.

How competitions work

At an international level, competitions are overseen by the International Council for Competition Climbing. This body represents participating nations, sets the rules, and organizes venues and dates for the World Series. National and regional competitions are organized by each country's ruling body, local clubs, and climbing walls.

There are several different types of competition, such as bouldering, speed climbing, and technical difficulty (in which climbers lead routes "on-sight", with no prior knowledge of the route). There are four categories in these contests: junior men, junior women, senior men, and senior women.

A competition comprises several rounds of increasing difficulty. Scoring is judged on the height gained at each round, so that gradually climbers are eliminated from the competition, leaving only a few at the final round. The winner is the climber who completes the final route, or reaches the highest point before falling off.

At the beginning of each round, climbers look at the route and can take notes. They then go into isolation and await their turn to climb. During isolation, climbers warm up so that they can achieve their maximum potential on the climb. After their attempt, climbers can watch the remainder of the round.

Competition tips

Once you have chosen which competition to enter, take note of the following hints and tips:

- Train sensibly and time it so that you are at peak fitness on the day. Rest well the day prior to the event.

- Make sure that you are warmed up and have plenty of liquid to stay hydrated throughout.

- Read the route or problem carefully before setting foot on it. Try to imagine yourself doing the moves, and don't get angry if you fail.

bouldering skills

Bouldering is one of the most enjoyable ways to improve both strength and skill.

Most bouldering problems are short and explosive, so will go only a little way to increasing your endurance. You will normally attempt technically difficult moves and sequences much harder than anything you might attempt on the crag.

Through the variety of climbing styles encountered when bouldering, you will learn many techniques that might otherwise take years of experience. For example, you'll learn about body tension on overhanging rock where abdominal and lower back muscles play an important role. You'll also improve your knowledge of differing handholds – crimps, slopers, and pinches among some of the more exotic – and how to use them when all else seems impossible.

You'll be able to focus on working out sequences of moves, knowing that you will not injure yourself if you fall off. However, as with any kind of training make sure that you gradually build up to harder problems to avoid tweaking muscles and tendons.

continued >

Avoiding common injuries
The strenuous nature of bouldering means that your body is at a higher risk of injury than other styles of climbing. Be aware of the following tips and hints:

• Finger-tape can be wrapped around fingers to prevent damage to tendons. This is a preventative measure rather than a solution.

• Warming up before climbing reduces the risk of muscle and tendon damage (see pages 130–31).

• To avoid long-term or serious injury to elbows and shoulders, follow a programme that allows you to build strength and stamina steadily.

• Ensure that there are rest days built in to your training programme.

Bouldering continued

The routes that boulderers climb are known as "problems" because they are usually short, can be perplexing, and the overall aim is to perfect the sequence of moves that solves the problem. The following problem incorporates three versatile bouldering techniques that will come in very useful when you come to attempt bouldering problems yourself.

1 The sit-down start
This problem begins with a sit-down start, which is a very common technique used in bouldering. By starting at ground level you maximize the number of moves, particularly on short problems.

2 The heel hook
In his first move the climber reaches for reasonably good handholds then swings one foot up to hook over an edged foothold just above the lip of the overhang. This is known as a heel hook. It helps the climber distribute some of his body weight on the leg and foot by keeping it under tension. You'll need strong stomach muscles to get into this position.

Planning ahead

When you approach a problem, envisage how to make the sequence of moves. Here, climbers work together to decide which holds to use and how.

3 The toe roll

The right foot is contorted around the lip of the overhang to gain extra purchase. The climber pulls on both arms and uses tension from the heel hook and leverage from the toe of the right foot to roll up onto the slab. This move is called a toe-roll. It is physically demanding but over relatively quickly.

4 Finishing the move

The handholds are sloping so the climber tries to keep below them, with the hand and arm smearing the rock. Once the body weight is transferred to the left foot, the right hand will be moved into a pushing position and a hard push from hand and leg will be used to stand up.

linking strenuous moves

An important aspect of improving your climbing technique is learning how to link strenuous sequences of moves. The key to this is good muscle strength and the ability to move quickly over rock, which will both take time to develop. Attempting routes or boulder problems on steep and overhanging sections of rock are both excellent ways to develop these skills.

1 Steep rock
On this steep, strenuous route, the climber uses holds in an imaginative and efficient way. To begin, a large hold for the right hand takes most of his weight.

2
He reaches another jug with his left hand. The right foot is flagged out to the right to maintain balance, and the outside edge of the left foot is used to assist.

3
The right foot is heel-hooked into a crack to help hold the climber into the rock, while he uses a free hand to clip into a running belay.

Overhanging rock

The climber uses an undercut pinch-grip hold to support his weight while he swings his feet across to the next footholds. He grips the right-hand hold with a slight sideways pull, so he can move his left hand across to a large hold. This movement requires body tension through powerful stomach muscles that help the climber to hold body and feet in a strong position.

4 The next move is a high step, made by leaning to the left on good holds. It is a dynamic move, but having protection nearby focuses the mind on the moves rather than a potential fall.

5 The climber pulls on handholds and pushes off with his feet to reach for a large hold for his right hand.

6 He moves into a resting position on the large hold, which is held at arm's length in a strong position.

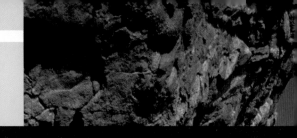

solo climbing

Solo climbing is climbing totally alone without rope, running belays, or safety protection. The risks are obvious – a fall can lead to death or serious injury. The appeal to the few experienced climbers who participate is a speedy, unimpeded style of climbing.

Solo climbing is not to everyone's liking – it may appear exhilarating, but beginners are advised to stay away from it. It is an area of climbing that should only be attempted after extensive experience of roped and technical climbing.

Deep-water soloing

A style of solo climbing that has become very popular is deep-water soloing (dubbed DWS by those in the know). Routes are climbed on rock above very deep water so that if the climber falls they fall

into relative safety. The climber must ensure that they don't hit anything on the way down, and that the water below is deep enough and clear of rocks.

Some DWS routes are quite outrageous in the severity of the climb and the diversity of the rock covered. Many routes are on a par with the hardest traditional routes and bouldering problems.

DWS routes can also reach quite dizzying heights – climbs of 30 m (100 ft) have been ascended, where if you fall you'll have plenty of time to think about your entry before hitting the water. In fact more often than not, the climb will finish below the top of the crag, and a leap into the sea is a mandatory way to finish.

Smith Rock

Oregon, USA

A beautiful wilderness area in the north-western United States, Smith Rock State Park offers a whole host of great climbs from mid grades upwards. The route below is Karate Crack, graded 5.10a – a classic three star route.

The climbing The rock is a type of fine sandstone known as "welded tuff" and offers truly remarkable features. The area is particularly noted for technical face climbing. There are around 1,400 climbs on varied crags within the park.

Kit Take a mixed trad rack and 60 m rope. Some climbs are protected by a mix of trad gear and bolts. There are a number of multi-pitch routes.

Getting there Fly to Portland then on to Bend. From there you can travel by bus to Smith Rock State Park.

When to go Spring and early Autumn are the best times; mid-summer can reach 38°C (100°F) despite the altitude.

Yosemite

California, USA

Yosemite has long multi-pitch and multi-day routes, as well as shorter climbs. To get the best from the valley you'll need to be climbing at mid- to upper grades; there are easier climbs around but the best tend to be harder.

The climbing The rock is exclusively granite, with big walls, slabs, and long cracks.

Kit Take a trad rack and 60 m rope, plus a second 60 m rope if you plan to abseil. You may need several nuts and cams of similar sizes for crack climbs. Multi-day routes require haul bags with food, water, and portaledges for sleeping on.

Getting there Fly to San Francisco, then drive to Yosemite, or catch a bus (journey time 3–4 hours). Alternatively, fly to Fresno for a shorter drive to Yosemite.

When to go End of April to mid-October. In summer, temperatures are high so Tuolomne Meadows (at high altitude) is a good venue.

The Cape

There are many climbing areas scattered around the Cape, from soaring routes on Table Mountain (such as Jacob's Ladder, graded 16, pictured below) to bouldering at Rocklands, and steep, multi-pitch climbing at Wolfberg.

The climbing The rock type varies all over the Cape and includes granite, quartzite, and incredibly solid sandstone. The whole area abounds with climbs of all grades from beginner's routes to the very hardest.

Kit Take a full trad rack with a good selection of nuts, cams, and hexes, and a 60 m rope. Double ropes are useful on some of the longer climbs.

Getting there Fly directly to Cape Town. A car is essential to reach most climbing areas.

When to go The best weather is from October to February. It can be very stormy during the winter (July and August).

Hampi

A unique bouldering venue in a historically significant region of India, Hampi is now a World Heritage Site. Granite boulders of all sizes abound and are scattered over a massive area. Visit for scenery and culture as much as the climbing.

The climbing The granite rock offers all types of bouldering, from thin face-cracks to thuggy, overhanging problems. Some of the larger boulders have bolted climbs.

Kit Take a bouldering mat, chalk, and shoes. You'll need a rope and harness plus a few quickdraws to climb the bolted routes.

Getting there Fly to Mumbai or Bangalore then catch a train or bus to Hampi. It is also possible to fly to an airstrip at nearby Hospet. Combine it with a visit to Goa for more bouldering and beach activity.

When to go December or January – it's too hot or rainy for climbing in other months.

Costa Daurada

Catalunya, Spain

The Costa Daurada centres on the Sierra de Prades mountains, and is home to bolted routes of all grades. La Rambla (9a) is one of the hardest climbs in the world; La Primera de l'estui, pictured below, is a classic route graded at 6b+.

The climbing The rock is limestone and in places has a vivid orange colour. The area is large so a car is useful if you plan to visit different areas. The main venues are Siurana and La Mussara.

Kit Take a 60 m rope with you, although 70 m will be more versatile. Since all routes are sport climbs, a rack of quickdraws and slings is all the protection you'll need.

When to go Because the Costa Daurada is a mountainous area, conditions for climbing are best from the end of April to mid-October.

Getting there Fly to Barcelona or Reus and drive to the climbing areas.

Lundy Island

Situated in the Bristol Channel, Lundy Island offers some of the best sea-cliff climbing in the UK. To get the most from the island you will need to be climbing at VS grade or above. The route below is Jet Set, graded E2 5c.

The climbing The rock type is very rough granite, but can be lichenous in places.

Kit Take a full trad rack with lots of variety, and double ropes. Consider taking a separate low-stretch abseil rope, as many of the routes require abseil access.

When to go Best conditions are from late April to the end of September, although poor weather is always possible.

Getting there Lundy Island is privately owned by the National Trust, and visitor numbers are limited. Access is via ferry or helicopter from Bideford on the Devon coast.

climbing on the net

Listed below is a small selection of climbing websites from around the world, containing everything from gear reviews, latest news, and articles, to crag descriptions, route guides, and location maps.

UK and IRELAND resources

www.ukclimbing.com
This is an excellent website for mostly UK-based climbers. but it also has lots of climbing news from around the world. It contains a superb crag locator, and also has weather forecasts and location maps. Good forum.

www.rockfax.com
A valuable resource with a route database for finding route information, this site contains downloadable topo maps for crags in the US and Europe. Also available are bouldering and climbing guidebooks for the UK, Spain, Norway and the US. The site also has a lively forum.

www.thebmc.co.uk
The British Mountaineering Council (BMC) is the body that represents climbers in the UK. The website is an excellent resource for UK and world news, and also contains access information, competition climbing listings, a route database, and climbing wall locations.

www.climbinfo.co.uk
A great website containing route information, a list of guides and instructors, latest news, new routes and links to stores.

www.planetfear.com
A lively website with lots of news and interest for climbers in the UK and around world. Plenty going on and a great resource.

US and CANADA resources

www.climbing.com
The website of Climbing magazine, this is a great news website and contains lots of action and gear reviews.

www.rockclimbing.com
Contains information from around the world, with excellent coverage of climbing in the US.

www.supertopo.com
This website contains free route guides, lots of bouldering information and great photos.

AUSTRALIA and NEW ZEALAND resources

www.climbing.com.au
This website has great crag information with a summary of recommended routes. Also includes details of clubs and accommodation.

www.thecrag.com
An online database of route information for crags in Australia and all over the world.

SOUTH AFRICA resources

www.climb.co.za
Everything you need to know about climbing in South Africa – from articles and latest news to topos and image galleries.

rock talk

Abseil – to descend on a rope using a friction device attached to a harness.

Anchor – to secure yourself to the rock face in order to belay a leader or a second. You can use single or multiple anchors.

Belay – the method of holding the rope used to safeguard a climber while he or she is climbing.

Belay device – the device that you hold the rope with to help you safeguard a climber.

Belay loop – the sewn loop on a harness linking the waistbelt and leg loops together.

Bolt – man-made permananent protection, usually drilled and glued into the rock face.

Bottom-roping – safeguarding a climber from the ground. The rope passes through a pulley style anchor at the top of the climb.

Bouldering – a low-level form of climbing and a sport in its own right.

Camming devices – a device used to secure a running belay or anchor in a crack in the rock.

Chalk up – to put chalk on your fingers and hands to help you get a better grip on the rock.

Dead rope – when belaying, the rope held by the belayer that doesn't go directly to the climber. Sometimes called the "controlling rope".

Delicate climbing – sometimes called "thin" climbing. The holds are tiny and precise and good technique is required.

Free climbing – climbing a route using only natural rock holds for hands and feet. Climbers are normally roped together.

Gear loop – the loops on a harness to which you can clip your gear.

HMS – a type of screwgate karabiner that is well-shaped for belaying. Stands for the original German "Halbmastwurfsicherung".

Leader – the climber who ascends the route first, placing gear as they go.

Live rope – when belaying, the rope that goes directly to the climber that you are belaying.

Lower-off – the fixed point at the top of a sport climb from which you lower to the ground. Also used to describe lowering a climber off a climb.

Nuts – wedge or hexagon-shaped pieces of metal on wire, rope, or tape that are wedged into cracks to make running belays or anchors.

On sight – to climb a route without any prior knowledge and without falling off.

Pay out – to feed rope through a belay device to allow the climber to continue a climb.

Prusik – a knot formed using a thin cord loop wrapped around the main climbing rope, such as the French Prusik, used in abseil safety.

Red point – to practise a climb by leading, and then to climb it again from the ground up in a single push. Usually the protection equipment is left in place.

Rest – to take a break on a climb. Usually so you can take one or both hands off the rock.

Running belay – protection arranged by the leader using wedge-shaped nuts, hexagon-shaped nuts, slings, camming devices, or bolts.

Second – the climber who follows the leader up the climb.

Solo – to climb alone and without any safety equipment whatsoever.

Sport climbing – a style of climbing where the protection for the leader is in place permanantly.

Stance – a place part way up a climb or at the top where you secure yourself whilst belaying.

Taking in – the gathering up of the slack rope by the leader while the second climbs up.

Top-roping – a style of climbing where the climber is belayed from the top of the climb. The belayer walks around to the top to make the anchor and create the stance.

Trad climbing – the purest form of climbing. All protection is placed by the lead climber, and is removed by the second, as they ascend.

Thuggy climbing – steep climbing, usually with big holds and potentially very strenuous.

index

and finally...

Thanks from the author
I'd like to thank Miranda Meilleur, Adam Hocking, and Bryn Williams for patiently giving their time to pose for photographs on the delightful cragging island of Sardinia. For clothing and backpacks for the photoshoot I am grateful to Mountain Hardwear, and technical equipment was kindly supplied by Wild Country. They also provided us with Red Chilli rock shoes and Infinity ropes. First Ascent kindly loaned Black Diamond helmets, and Salomon GB supplied us with approach shoes. Ray Wood provided us with inspirational images for the destinations sections. Your generosity and kindness is much appreciated!

Thanks from Dorling Kindersley
DK would like to thank Letty Luff for editorial assistance, Thomas Keenes and David Garvin for design assistance, and Margaret McCormack for indexing.

Thanks for the pictures
The publisher would like to thank the following for their kind permission to reproduce their photographs: Nigel Shepherd: 4–5, 8–9, 23, 29bl, 29br, 30br, 30–31t, 32tl, 32br, 33b, 37tr, 37bl, 128, 129br, 147, 148, 150, 151, 153, 156–157, 158–159; Ray Wood Photography: 136, 137, 144, 146, 149.

But be careful...
Rock climbing is potentially hazardous – all participants must assume responsibility for their own actions and safety. Neither the author nor the publisher can be held responsible for any accidents resulting from following any of the activities shown in this book. Always prepare for the unexpected and be cautious.